Organization Theory

SAGE COURSE COMPANIONS

KNOWLEDGE AND SKILLS *for* SUCCESS

Organization Theory

Ann L. Cunliffe

SAGE Publications

Los Angeles ▪ London ▪ New Delhi ▪ Singapore

First published 2008

SAGE Publications Ltd
1 Oliver's Yard
55 City Road
London EC1Y 1SP

SAGE Publications Inc.
2455 Teller Road
Thousand Oaks, California 91320

SAGE Publications India Pvt Ltd
B 1/I 1 Mohan Cooperative Industrial Area
Mathura Road
New Delhi 110 044

SAGE Publications Asia-Pacific Pte Ltd
33 Pekin Street #02-01
Far East Square
Singapore 048763

Library of Congress Control Number: 2007930329

British Library Cataloguing in Publication data

A catalogue record for this book is available from
the British Library

ISBN 978-1-4129-3548-7
ISBN 978-1-4129-3549-4 (pbk)

Typeset by C&M Digitals (P) Ltd, Chennai, India
Printed in India by Replika Press Pvt. Ltd
Printed on paper from sustainable resources

contents

contents

How to Use the Book

This book provides a concise summary of the main topics, theories and issues in organization theory (OT). It also provides guidelines on how to make sense of course material, why it is important, and how to apply the theories and concepts to the design and management of organizations. It does not replace your textbook or lectures, which will go into the various aspects of organization theory in more detail, but it is designed as a supplementary text to be used to facilitate learning and enable you to get the most from your textbook and lectures. It also provides you with essential help revising for your course exams, preparing and writing course assessment materials, and enhancing your knowledge and thinking skills in line with course requirements. You may want to glance through it quickly, reading it in parallel with your course syllabus, and note where each topic is covered in both the syllabus and the Companion. The Companion will help you to anticipate exam questions and gives guidelines on what your examiners will be looking for. It should be seen as a framework in which to organize the subject matter, and to extract the most important points from your textbooks, lecture notes and other learning materials on your course.

There are a number of textbooks on organization theory and not all of them take the same approach. Some deal with OT from a systems and contingency perspective (e.g., Child, 2005; Daft, 2007; Jones, 2007), some take a critical or postmodern perspective (Hassard and Parker, 1993) or a multiple perspectives approach (Hatch with Cunliffe, 2006; Morgan, 1997; Scott, 1992). Your textbook might be an edited volume, with chapters written by different authors (e.g., Clegg and Hardy, 1998; Reed and Hughes, 1992). It's impossible to cover all of the variations in this Course Companion. But we will focus on what is generally regarded as mainstream OT based on structuralist (organizations as objects) and contingency approaches, which formed the bulk of organization theory (and still does in the US) until 20 years ago, when European organization theorists began to explore different perspectives. This work addresses critical issues in organizations and organization theory, previously unconsidered: gender, race, ethnicity, the relationship between knowledge and power, organizations as socially constructed rather than objective entities, technoscience, the role and legitimacy of organizations in society, Marxist critiques, and so on. We will look at some of these contemporary approaches to OT in each chapter. If you are using a structuralist contingency-based book, this might whet your appetite to look at alternative approaches. If you are using a non-structuralist contingency book, this might help you make sense of some quite challenging concepts and ideas! Whichever textbook you are using, this Course Companion will help you fit all the pieces together and understand how OT actually applies to 'real' organizations. Whichever textbook you are using, the basics are the basics: read the Companion in parallel with your textbook and identify where subjects are covered in more detail in both your text and in your course syllabus.

Having taught Organization Theory for over 20 years to both undergraduate and graduate students, I understand the problems, issues and concerns that students have about the topic. These include: OT is an overly theoretical subject; that there is a lot of information to grasp; that the terminology is confusing; and that OT has no practical relevance. The book addresses these concerns, and is designed around my experience of what you need to know to get the most from your course, deal with the problems you might encounter in trying to understand OT, and help you navigate the course assessment process. So use it as a study guide.

Part 2 relates specifically to organization theory. It provides a framework for understanding the field, reviews the essentials of OT, and offers a way of integrating the various topics. Each section takes one or more of the main topics covered in OT textbooks, and focuses on: 'What do I need to know about *[the topic]* – and why?'

In order to answer this question, the sections cover:

1 Key concepts: a summary of the main theories, key themes, issues and what you need to know about the topic. How these fit together to help managers understand, design and manage organizations more effectively. Practical examples to aid your understanding and emphasize how managers use, or could use, the theoretical material.

2 Contemporary approaches: current ideas and different approaches and theories relating to the topic.

3 An integrative case: to help make the concepts more meaningful and help you understand how to apply them.

4 Using the material: study tips and potential essay questions with ideas about how to answer them.

5 Taking it further: Key questions, alternative approaches and debates on the topic.

You can use Part 2 in one of two ways, and this will depend on your preferred method of studying. You might find it helpful to read each section *before* you read your textbook and attend class or seminars. This will give you an overview of the topic prior to getting into the more detailed material in your textbook. Sometimes, if you understand the overall context and why the topic is important, it's easier to fit in the details. A second approach might be to read your textbook first, and *then* read this book, to help you pull out the key issues and apply the concepts. Find the approach that makes most sense to *you*.

Part 3 provides some great information on study skills in general: how to organize yourself to get the most out of lectures, to contribute effectively to seminars, and how to study for and write papers and exams. It's a good idea to read Part 3 before your course starts, because then you can be proactive in managing your learning process. It will make life much easier! There then follows a glossary of terms and references.

Before we jump into our introduction to organization theory, I want to offer a general guideline that I give to all of my OT students:

> Keep up with your reading as assigned by your instructor – there is a lot of material, and if you get behind it's difficult to catch up. Your lectures will also make a lot more sense if you know what the main theories and ideas are before you attend. And if you don't understand any of them – you can then ask.

What is Organization Theory (OT) and Why Study It?

OT is a range of theories and models that attempt to explain how organizations function and relate to the environment. The driving force behind OT is the idea that if we understand this, then we can design organizations in such a way that they operate:

- efficiently – utilizing their resources in a cost-effective way
- effectively – achieving their goals
- responsibly – in a way that respects the community, society and the environment.

OT differs from organizational behaviour (OB) in three main ways: OT focuses on organizations – OB on people in organizations; OT takes a macro organizational perspective – OB looks at more micro behavioural processes; OT is concerned with structures, systems and processes – OB with the perceptions and behaviour of individuals and groups.

The term 'organization' implies that there is some sort of structure and order to the way things are done, and definitions often centre around the idea that organizations are entities in which individuals coordinate their actions to achieve specific goals. They can be small family-owned businesses or multinational corporations, for-profit or non-profit, private or public, service or product oriented, government agencies...We experience organizations on a daily basis as we go to college, buy a house, travel on holiday, eat in a restaurant, or visit a hospital. However, even though we come into contact with various parts of an organization (customer service, administration, accounting, etc.), we probably don't think about how these parts work together, unless we have a problem – when we don't receive the expected service, or the product we've purchased is faulty – which means something in the organization isn't functioning the way it should be.

Many students think OT is a particularly theoretical and abstract discipline, when in fact it's quite the opposite. Many of the theories are based on studies of what happens in organizations, so they are grounded in practice. And even though they may not be aware of it, managers use organization theory every day as they think about ways of organizing the work in their department (*division of labour*), about how the work needs to be coordinated with work in other departments (**integration**), about how to create a work environment that encourages organizational members to work together towards goals (*culture*), and so on. But unless they have studied OT, they might not have the explicit and systematic knowledge to enable them to do this in the most effective way. So OT gives managers a range of theories, concepts, models and tools that they can use to diagnose problems and help their department and organization function more effectively.

It's particularly important for managers to understand the various elements involved in designing effective organizations – how to create a structure and culture that balance external and internal demands allows the organization to create value, and ensures its long-term survival. Ineffective organization structure reduces productivity and competitiveness, and can lead to low morale as employees struggle to achieve their goals. An effective organization structure and design allows organizational members to do the following:

- Deal with contingencies such as changing technology, markets and competition.
- Gain a competitive advantage by developing the core competencies and strategies to enable them to outperform other companies.
- Work in an effective, supportive and responsive environment.
- Increase efficiency and innovation.

Let's begin with an example.

You own and manage a restaurant in your local town, which can seat up to 80 people, and is open for lunch and dinner. You serve an international cuisine, the price range of an entrée is moderate to high, and you offer elegant décor and a romantic atmosphere. You employ a staff of 30 people, which includes an Assistant Manager, chef and cooks, bar staff, waitpersons, cleaner and a cashier.

There is currently no real competition, with only a McDonald's and a Chinese restaurant in the town, but you hear rumours that there may be a new chain restaurant opening soon…

You are already using organization theory in considering:

1 What's going on in terms of legal requirements, the national and local economy, competition, the availability of a skilled labour pool, etc., that might affect your restaurant (i.e., *the environment*).

2 How to best organize the work and coordinate the activities of your employees to make sure your customers enjoy their dining experience and return again and again (*structure and design*).

3 What equipment you need, and how to design your restaurant layout so that you are using the space you have most efficiently and aesthetically. In other words, waitstaff have easy access to customers and the kitchen, and customers find the dining atmosphere and experience a pleasant one (*technology*).

4 How you want staff to interact with each other and the customers (*culture*).

5 How you are going to manage the organization (*power, control, decision making, making changes*).

We will use this example throughout the book to illustrate the concepts in each chapter and to show how you can apply them in organizations.

Studying Organization Theory

When teaching OT, I emphasize three issues that students find helpful:

- We are studying individual topics, but everything is interrelated.
- No theory is complete, no one theory applies in every situation, nor is it an accurate description of the way organizations really are – theory is a lens or framework for viewing the world.
- When reading about the theories, think about how they might apply to organizations with which you are familiar – either as an employee, a customer, a student or a volunteer.

Interrelatedness

Whichever textbook you are reading, and whoever is teaching the course, you will be studying OT as a number of topics, perspectives or issues. It's important to keep in mind that even though you might be studying these separately, everything interrelates. One way of thinking about OT is as a jigsaw puzzle in which all the pieces have to fit to form the whole picture.

So while you might be discussing one aspect of OT per class – structure, control, environment – try to relate the topics to each other. For example, the organization's environment will influence which structure will be most effective; structure and culture are closely linked; the forms of control that are most appropriate will depend on the structure and culture, and so on. As we work through each topic we will emphasize this interconnectivity. OT starts to make sense from both a theoretical and a practical perspective when you understand that everything needs to fit together for an organization to be effective.

Theory as a lens

Also, remember that while many of the theories are based on actual studies of organizations, they offer a lens, or way of thinking about organizations, rather than describing the way organizations *really* function. In other words theories are a researcher's (or a group of researchers') way of analysing what they see. You will find that different theories will offer different ways of thinking about the same issue, some are contradictory, and some might be more helpful than others when trying to understand an organization you are studying or are working in. Each organization

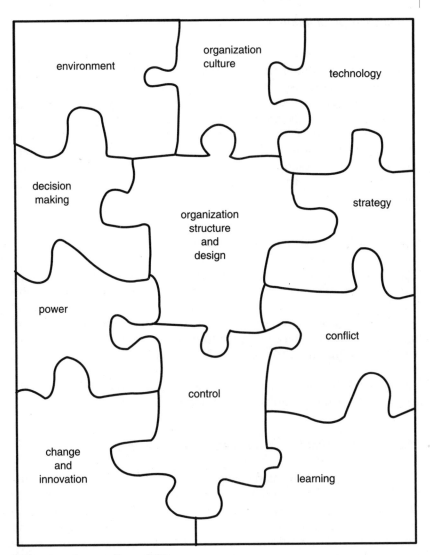

Figure 1   An overview of OT

operates under its own unique set of circumstances. Theories are most useful if you use different ones to give you different perspectives on what might be happening in your organization. This is the value of OT – by using different lenses you will broaden your understanding about how organizations can be designed and managed in more effective ways.

The application of theories

Finally, as you read your textbook, look for practical examples of the ideas you are studying. If you are currently employed, think about how the theories relate to your own organization. If you are a full-time student, think about your experience as a customer, a patient or a client. Look for examples of various organizations on the Internet. Most large companies have their own websites, which include information on their goals, vision statements, business strategy and policy statements (e.g. social responsibility). In each section I will suggest further resources – so check these out, they can make abstract concepts more real.

A Brief History of Organization Theory

Organization Theory has a long history and draws on a number of academic disciplines; sociology, economics, political science, philosophy. Your textbook may or may not discuss the history of OT, but it is important in giving you an overview of work in the field, and in understanding why OT scholars take different approaches. Table 1 summarizes the main approaches, their focus, key scholars and the main principles you need to know.

Early work in the field was not classified as Organization Theory, because OT wasn't recognized as a discipline until the 1960s.

Classical and scientific management (1900 onwards)

Classical and scientific management perspectives emerged at a time when big business was growing along with a concern for increasing efficiency through the standardization of production. They draw on the work of both academics (sociologists, administrative theorists and economists) and practitioners interested in finding ways to manage organizations more efficiently. *Classical management* theory aims to find the 'one best way' to manage through the application of scientific methods and universal principles. Two main contributors to the classical approach are Fayol (1919/1949) and Weber (1924/1947). Taylor (1911) is regarded as the founder of scientific management. Both of these approaches are still in evidence in today's organizations.

Fayol (a French CEO) listed the functions of management as planning, organizing, coordinating, commanding and controlling. He also

Table 1   A brief summary of the history of OT

	Authors	Focus	Main principles
Classical & Scientific Management (1900 →)	Smith (1776) Marx (1867) Taylor (1911) Fayol (1919/1949) Weber (1924/1947)	The role of organizations on society, the influence on work and workers (sociological). The most efficient structure, way of organizing (people and work) and managing, based on scientific principles.	Clear division of labour and routine work. Formalization. Hierarchy and managerial authority. Standardization. One best way.
Systems & Contingency Theories (Modernism) (1950 →)	Parsons (1951) Gouldner (1954) Boulding (1956) March & Simon (1958) Woodward (1965) Trist and Bamforth (1951) Burns and Stalker (1966) Lawrence and Lorsch (1967)	The need to study organizations as complex systems with interrelated parts. Utilizes an input–output model. Contingency theory emphasizes there is no 'one best way' and suggests that management and organizational practices will depend on the characteristics of each situation.	All parts need to fit to optimize efficiency. Balance inputs and outputs. System needs to adapt to changing environment Environment: stable/unstable Structure: mechanistic/organic Culture: control/commitment Technology: routine/complex
Social Construction (1960s →)	Berger and Luckmann (1966) Goffman (1959) Boje (1991) Law (1994) Weick (1969/1979; 1995)	Organizational realities are constructed in social interaction, through shared meanings, artifacts, symbols, stories etc. We need to study organizations as social, historical and linguistic processes.	Enactment, sensemaking. Organizations as communities. Technology as processes of social construction and structuration.
Postmodernism (1980 →)	Foucault (1973) Lyotard (1984) Harvey (1990) Cooper and Burrell (1988) Hassard and Parker (1993)	Questioning mainstream ideas of organizations, their purpose, their form, how they operate. Uncovering assumptions about what is right and acceptable, to expose inequalities and oppression.	Organizations are systems of power relations, where some groups are oppressed by others. Organizations are arenas of disorder, conflict and contradiction.

identified 14 principles of management he believed would lead to organizational efficiency and effectiveness. These included:

- Unity of command: one person – one boss
- Authority: the right to give orders
- Discipline: obedience, respect

Max Weber (a German sociologist) also addressed the issue of structure in his *theory of bureaucracy* – an organization structure in which members work according to pre-set, standardized rules and procedures. He identified a number of principles of a bureaucratic organization that would ensure fairness and rationality:

- Rational-legal authority: authority based on position not on individual factors.
- Decisions and positions based on technical competence.
- A hierarchy of authority and responsibility with clearly specified descriptions.
- Clear vertical chain of command.
- Formal written rules and procedures to control performance, with training in job requirements.
- Written records, rules, policies, procedures, etc.
- Impersonal relationships among career professionals.

You will probably find reference to Weber's work in the sections on organization structure and design because these principles often underlie functional structures, and are prevalent in government organizations. In the US, the staffing operation of the federal government is based on the Merit System, which specifies how all aspects of human resource management should be carried out – hiring, job classification, promotion, discipline, etc.

Taylor's (1911) notion of *scientific management* focused on the most efficient way to manage. He believed that the goal of management should be to secure the maximum prosperity for both the employer and employee, and that this could be achieved by applying scientific principles to work methods and to management. He stated that managers need to analyse work using scientific methods, select, train and develop workers for each job, cooperate with the workers to ensure the work is being done correctly, that managers should manage and workers work, i.e., workers should have no control. Over time, his ideas had a worldwide impact on organizations and management. Prior to Taylor's book, there had been no real published formalized guidelines for managing organizations and work – scientific management offered a systematic approach that managers could apply to their own organization.

Systems theory (1950 onwards)

Systems theory offers a way of studying how organizations function, and is a model used by a number of OT textbooks. The organization is represented as an *open system*, which is goal oriented, and operates as an input–output model transforming resources such as money and materials into products or services. As a system, the organization has a number of characteristics:

- An *open system* continually adapts to changes in the environment.
- It consists of a number of interdependent subsystems (functions, departments, processes such as decision making, information, production) that interact to form the whole.
- It strives for equilibrium, balancing its inputs and outputs to maintain a steady flow of activity.
- It creates feedback mechanisms to enable this process to occur.

You can usually identify systems theories if they talk about interrelated subsystems, feedback mechanisms, adaptation, etc. One variation, *socio-technical systems* theory, emphasizes the role of people in the system. The work of the Tavistock Institute (UK), in particular Trist and Bamforth's (1951) study of the British coal mining industry, has been influential in drawing attention to the relationship between technology, social relationships, morale and performance. They suggested (back in the 1950s!) that autonomous work groups may not be the most technically efficient way of organizing work, but led to higher productivity and worker satisfaction. Woodward (1965) continued this work in the area of technology and organizational design.

Contingency theory (1960s onwards)

Contingency theory emphasizes there is no 'one best way' (as in the classical and scientific management approaches) and suggests that management and organizational practices will depend on the characteristics of each situation. In other words, finding the appropriate organization structure will depend on many factors including the environment, the task and technology, people etc. You will come across a number of *contingency-based studies* in your textbook, especially looking at the relationship between the environment, organization structure and design, technology and strategy. Look for the phrase, 'in X set of circumstances/particular situation – then Y will be most appropriate, in M – then N will apply...', because this is often an indication that a contingency approach is being used.

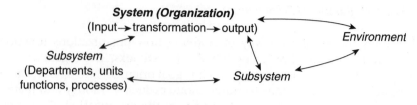

Figure 2   An open systems approach to OT

While these approaches have been a major part of OT for years, and still are (especially in the US), there are more contemporary perspectives to consider. Some textbooks (e.g., Child, 2005; Daft, 2007; Jones, 2007) do not address these because they explicitly take a systems and contingency approach. Others (e.g., Hatch with Cunliffe, 2006; Morgan, 1997; Watson, 2006) incorporate contemporary perspectives. Whether your textbook does or doesn't, you may be interested in reading about them because they do offer different ways of thinking about organizations.

Why different perspectives?

Let's go back to 1979 and the publication of a book by British organization theorists Gibson Burrell and Gareth Morgan called *Sociological Paradigms and Organizational Analysis*. This book had a major impact on the discipline because the authors claimed that scholars actually took different and often competing approaches to the study of OT based on their assumptions about the nature of science (e.g., is reality real or is it created in the ways we talk about the world, are we free-willed individuals or are our lives determined by the environment?) and the nature of society (is society characterized by unity and consensus or conflict and change?). They suggested that studies of organizations could be placed in one of four *paradigms* (ways of viewing the world):

1 Functionalist: organizations as objects of rationality and efficiency, mainly structuralist and contingency approaches.

2 Interpretivist: organizations as emerging in social practices.

3 Radical humanist: the relationship between organizations and human consciousness (alienation, self-fulfillment, emancipation).

4 Radical structuralist: how organizations, managerial ideologies and systems of production oppress the working class.

This sparked an ongoing debate known as the paradigm wars as OT scholars argued for one paradigm over another. But despite being controversial, the book offered a way of mapping various approaches to organization theory and paved the way for alternative perspectives that added to the richness of the field. You will get a sense of what these perspectives have to offer as you read on...

Some perspectives to consider

Some textbooks, particularly those taking a multiple perspectives approach (e.g., Hatch with Cunliffe, 2006; Morgan, 1997), look at additional approaches to the main classical, systems and contingency approaches. Gareth Morgan's influential book, *Images of Organization* (1997) was one of the first books to draw attention to the need to study organizations from different perspectives. Morgan suggested that organization theories are based on metaphors, or ways of seeing the world. He identified eight metaphors:

1 Organizations as Machines: rational, efficient, hierarchical, mechanistic. Classical and scientific management.

2 Organizations as Organisms: open systems adapting to environmental demands. Systems and contingency theories.

3 Organizations as Brains: learning, sharing information and knowledge, questioning the ways in which things are done. Cybernetics.

4 Organizations as Cultures: with shared visions, values, rituals, stories, subcultures. Social constructionism and enactment.

5 Organizations as Political Systems: systems of power and conflict because of different interests and agendas.

6 Organizations as Psychic Prisons: involving the unconscious, patriarchy, repressed sexuality – both destructive and creative.

7 Organizations as Flux and Transformation: complex, non-linear, self-organizing systems characterized by contradiction. Chaos and complexity theory.

8 Organizations as Instruments of Domination: in which people are alienated, have to comply to corporate interests, are repressed and exploited. Marxist perspectives.

He suggested that by viewing organizations in this way we can see them differently and find new ways of designing and managing them.

Two other perspectives you may come across are social constructionist (or symbolic) and postmodern perspectives. Both of these require a philosophical understanding – because they think about the nature of reality and knowledge in very different ways. Classical, scientific management, systems and contingency approaches assume that reality exists independently from people, and that knowledge is based on identifying facts about what is happening and developing theories, general principles and models so that we can predict and manage what happens in the future. As you will see if you read further, social constructionist and postmodern perspectives are based on a different set of assumptions and different ways of viewing organizations. Your textbook may not cover these perspectives – but you might find they offer interesting ways of thinking about organizations!

Social constructionist approaches (1960s onwards)

Social constructionist-based work has become increasingly popular within organization studies over the last 20 years. The story began with Berger and Luckmann's influential book *The Social Construction of Reality* (1966), in which they argued that social realities are created and maintained in social interaction and conversations with others, rather than in structures. The central theme of *social constructionism* is:

> 'Social objects are not given in the world but constructed, negotiated, reformed, fashioned, and organized by human beings in their efforts to make sense of happenings in the world.' (Sarbin and Kitsuse, 1994: 3)

Karl Weick (1969/1979; 1995) popularized social constructionist approaches to organization theory with his ideas about enactment and sensemaking. He suggested that managers enact organizations as they try to make sense of the uncertain situations they find themselves in. The organization and its structure, systems and processes don't exist as objects separate from people – they are created as organizational members talk about what they think is happening and what needs to be done. So organizing is really a sensemaking activity – as organizational members try to make sense of their surroundings, they form mental images or maps that highlight particular aspects of their experience. When these are shared they become part of what we think is our organizational reality. However, these features and images did not exist before – they are created by people in their conversations and other forms of communication.

If you are interested in this approach, in addition to Weick's work, you may want to read Boje (1991), Watson (2001), or Law's (1994) work. Tony Watson spent a year working alongside managers in an organization, and explores how they made sense of their experience and constructed their identities in their conversations. John Law studied how employees working in a laboratory tried to create organization and social order through stories, conversations, technology, written texts, buildings, etc.

Postmodern approaches (1980s onwards)

Postmodernism is a complex field of study drawing on the work of Karl Marx and critical theorists, and poststructuralist work in the area of language and philosophy. The latter draws on the work of Saussure (a linguist), Jean-Francois Lyotard, Michel Foucault (a French philosopher) and Jacques Derrida (another French philosopher). It is impossible to summarize all the main ideas of *postmodernism* for two main reasons: it requires an understanding of linguistics and philosophy, and postmodern ideas are wide ranging. So let me pick out some key ideas that underlie postmodern approaches to organization theory:

- There is no fixed, commonly understood, external social reality, only images, fragmented views and performances.
- Organizations are created and maintained in linguistic conventions (created by language not by people), simulations, arenas of conflict where some groups have power over, and oppress, other groups.
- Knowledge is not rational and universal. Knowledge does not lead to enlightened civilization and progress – but to the domination and marginalization of groups.
- Meanings are not fixed in words, but slip and slide depending on how they are used in particular contexts.
- We need to deconstruct 'texts' (readings, actions, organizations, etc.) to uncover different readings, hidden power relations, and how groups are marginalized and repressed.

Postmodernists argue that organizations are performances and simulations, characterized by uncertainty, complexity and contradiction.

As you can see, this is a very different way of looking at the purpose of organizations, the way they operate and their impact!

This brief historical foray sets the scene for the topics and theories you will encounter in your textbook, and will help explain why particular studies took the approach they did. So, as you work through each section and encounter different ideas and theories, see whether they take a scientific management approach (this is the best way), a systems approach (finding an optimum balance between inputs and outputs), a contingency approach (it all depends on...), a social constructionist approach (organizations are enacted in interaction and conversations), or a postmodern approach (organizations as fragmented and oppressive).

Before finishing this section I want to address one topic that will be covered in your textbook, but probably not in Chapter 1. I will explain why in the next section.

Decision Making

Many OT textbooks have a separate chapter on decision making, usually towards the end of the book. I've always found it easier to cover decision making in the first or second class because I can reinforce the learning points throughout the course as we discuss structure, strategy, etc. If your course includes case studies and group work, then you are often problem solving and making decisions in your group. So an understanding of the process of decision making can help put both case study content and your own approach to decision making in perspective. What are some of the key aspects of decision making? We will look at different types and approaches to decision making, and in the latter, consider the factors influencing the decision-making process.

Decision making is basically the process of making a choice from a variety of alternatives. It can occur in response to a problem, or it may relate to a desire to increase effectiveness or innovate. There are two types of decisions in an organization:

1 *Programmed*: decisions made on a regular basis with procedures, rules, or routines for dealing with them. For example, how to deal with employee complaints or grievances, how students apply for financial aid, the rules relating to educational reimbursement and tuition assistance for employees, operating procedures, and so on. The more decisions are programmable, the easier they are to deal

with. Bureaucracies thrive on programmed decisions because they ensure consistency, fairness and control. If the organization operates in a relatively stable environment, then decisions can be programmed because few new problems arise.

2 *Unprogrammed*: these are unique, one-off decisions for which there are no rules or procedures. These decisions require more effort and energy and the solution is by no means guaranteed. These may include developing new products, making strategic decisions about whether to diversify or move into new markets, and dealing with new unexpected operational problems. As you will see in the section on structure and design, matrix structures are designed to deal with unprogrammed decisions because they operate in changing environments.

Of course we like to think that both organizations and individuals make decisions on a rational basis, but this is not always the case, as you will see in the various models below.

The rational model

This model is based on the idea that a rational, step-by-step approach to problem solving and decision making will yield the optimum answer. *Rational models* vary in the number of steps they include, but generally these involve: identifying and defining the problem, getting facts and determining the goal, generating and evaluating alternative solutions, choosing the best alternative, implementing the decision, and evaluating its success. This can make the decision-making process more systematic, for example, we have a tendency to jump to generating solutions before we've really defined the problem or got all the information we need about the problem. If you are working on a case study in a group, think about how you analyse the case and arrive at recommendations – do you adopt a rational approach? However, we often find ourselves dealing with unprogrammed decisions, with constraints that might prevent us from getting all the information we need, or the outcomes may be so uncertain that it's difficult to evaluate alternatives. This leads us to the next model.

The Carnegie model

In the 1950s and 1960s, American administrative theorists James March, Herbert Simon and Richard Cyert developed the Carnegie model, which is based on the argument that the rational model doesn't really consider the realities of organizational decision making – that it is often subject to incomplete information, different perceptions and conflict over goals and resources. They suggested that the decision-making process involves:

1 *Satisficing*: managers don't (or can't) get all the facts, and they don't identify all the possible alternatives but use rules of thumb or select a satisfactory (not necessarily the optimum) solution. This is especially the case in unprogrammed decisions.

2 *Bounded rationality*: we are rational within the bounds of our perception, our knowledge, our experience, and the time we have available. This influences our ability to deal with complex problems and means that what is 'rational' will vary for each person.

3 *Coalitions:* organizational members with similar interests group together to influence the decision-making process in their favour. The final decision might reflect the interests of the most dominant alliance.

So the Carnegie model is suggesting that decision making is a political rather than a rational process – think of decisions made in your department and organization where negotiating occurred between people, and trade-offs made in return for support.

The incremental model

Henry Mintzberg argued that organizational decisions are not usually radically new or different, but are based on a number of small choices made at different times in response to different issues that emerge.

The garbage can model

Think of an organization as having a number of goals, problems, solutions, opportunities, problem solvers, coalitions, skills and expertise, all floating around. One day, a problem solver is tinkering around with some production equipment and discovers accidentally that a minor adjustment results in a major improvement in product quality. This is an example of the garbage can approach, which is based on the idea that decision making doesn't necessarily follow a logical sequence, but that solutions can be proposed before problems are identified, problems may persist without being solved, or a decision can be made that leads to problems. Of course this may or may not result in the best decision – but this form of decision making occurs and it's important to recognize when it works and when it doesn't.

As you read through the sections on strategy and organization structure, think about the types of decisions being made, and what structures might be best suited to deal with particular types of decisions. When you are analysing case studies, try to identify the types and approaches to decision making that are used in the case. And finally, think about your own approach to decision making when working on case studies; do you use a rational, Carnegie, garbage can approach? In all of these situations, the key is deciding whether the model being used is appropriate to the type of problem and situation being addressed. This brings us back to why we need to study OT – because it can give us the knowledge and tools to be able to evaluate whether the organization and organizational members are working in the most effective way.

USING THE MATERIAL

Even though this is an introduction and overview of OT, it can provide you with information you can use in discussions, case study analysis, papers and exams. Some typical questions you may be asked to consider include:

1 Why do managers need to understand organization theory?

When answering this question think not only of the general reasons we've identified in this section, but also look at the various OT topics such as structure, design, technology, power etc. and you will find reasons why managers need to understand each. Give examples of some of the theories that are useful and why.

2 Discuss how the various approaches (perspectives, metaphors) to organization theory can contribute to the design and management of organizations today.

The answer to this question will obviously depend on which textbook you are using: Morgan's metaphors, Hatch's perspectives, Scott's rational, natural and open systems etc. It's important to discuss how the different metaphors or perspectives or approaches highlight the limitations of seeing the world from one perspective and can help managers: 'read' situations differently; analyse complex situations more effectively; be open to alternative ways of thinking about, designing and managing organizations. Give examples of how different metaphors (etc.) can offer different views on particular issues or topics such as power or strategy.

3 'No decision is ever rational.' Discuss.

Talk about what the rational approach to decision making is; why it doesn't always work; what alternative approaches exist; and give examples of decisions where more creative approaches might need to be taken, or where a manager might satisfice or build coalitions.

In addition to answering specific questions on this material, you can incorporate it in essays on other topics as background material. I call this using material 'in passing' – it's not directly related to the topic or question but provides additional useful information. For example, in a paper on strategy you can mention that a particular decision is an example of unprogrammed decision making, or that senior managers appear to be taking a garbage can approach to decision making because… When analysing case studies you could take a contingency approach as an overall framework, or identify examples of coalitions, satisficing and programmed decision making. In other words, don't forget this material – use it when you can because it shows you understand how the different elements of OT relate to each other. When I see students incorporate these ideas, it shows me they are able to take an integrated and holistic perspective.

Taking it **FURTHER**

Given the different perspectives and theories in OT – some of which are contradictory – it's tempting to say that it offers nothing of value to managers. Is one perspective or theory any better than any other? Why can't we have one organization theory, an ideal structure, or a set of 'good' organization culture characteristics…? This would make life a lot simpler! But if you are currently working in an organization, you know that life is never simple and

(Continued)

there are always unanticipated occurrences. Organizations operate in an increasingly complex, competitive and changing environment, and managers often rapidly find themselves dealing with a whole range of issues and problems. So different perspectives and theories can help managers analyse these complex situations, and offer different ideas and options about how to deal with them. Keep an open mind, be flexible, and consider all options!

Textbook Guide

CHILD: *Chapter 1.*
DAFT: *Chapters 1 and 12.*
HATCH WITH CUNLIFFE: *Chapters 1, 2, and 10.*
JONES: *Chapters 1 and 12.*
WATSON: *Chapter 1.*

Additional Reading

Boje, D. M. (1991) 'The storytelling organization: a study of story performance in an office-supply firm', *Administrative Science Quarterly*, 36: 106–26.

Clegg, S. and Hardy, C. (eds) (1998) *Studying Organizations: Theory and Method*. London: Sage.

Foucault, M. (1973) *The Order of Things: An Archaeology of the Human Sciences* (trans. Alan Sheridan-Smith). New York: Vintage Books.

Gergen, K. J. (1992) 'Organization theory in the postmodern era', in M. Reed and M. Hughes (eds) *Rethinking Organization: New Directions in Organization Theory and Analysis*. London: Sage.

Goffman, E. (1959) *The Presentation of Self in Everyday Life*. Garden City, NY: Doubleday.

Hassard, J. and Parker, M. (eds) (1993) *Postmodernism and Organizations*. London: Sage.

Hatch, M. J. with Cunliffe, A. L. (2006) *Organization Theory: Modern, Symbolic, and Postmodern Perspectives,* 2nd edn. Oxford: Oxford University Press.

Law, J. (1994) *Organizing Modernity*. Oxford: Blackwell.

Morgan, G. (1997) *Images of Organization*, 2nd edn. Thousand Oaks, CA: Sage (originally published 1986).

Watson, T. J. (2001) *In Search of Management: Culture, Chaos and Control in Managerial Work*. London: Routledge.

Weick, Karl E. (1969/1979) *The Social Psychology of Organizing*. Reading, MA: Addison-Wesley (first published 1969).

Weick, K. E. (1995) *Sensemaking in Organizations*. Thousand Oaks, CA: Sage Publications.

part two
core areas of the curriculum

1	
organization structure and design	

A number of OT textbooks cover organization structure and design in separate chapters, but it's helpful to look at them together because organizational design relates to how you balance the various elements of organization structure. This aspect of OT can be particularly confusing, and you might find yourself grappling with the terminology and trying to figure out how all the various elements fit together. But persevere; it will make sense over time. As a way of helping you through this, we'll look at why organization structure and design are important, briefly define the key terms, identify the different types of organization structures, and discuss how organizational design differs in each.

The difference between organization structure and organizational design can be confusing. Think of structure as the organization's skeleton, the basic framework and shape of the organization usually represented in the organization chart. Organization design relates to the various elements that make up structure. If we continue the biological metaphor, then design is the respiratory, muscular, cardiovascular etc. systems that move things around the body and ensure it functions. Structure doesn't exist without design – and vice versa – and all the elements need to be coordinated and work together. *What* these elements are and the *way* they are coordinated (**organizational design**) relate to different organization structures. You might want to check out the websites of the organizations mentioned in the section for examples of different types of structures. These should help illustrate what these different structures look like in actuality. We will not focus on the advantages and disadvantages of each structure because most OT textbooks discuss these in a straightforward way. What we will look at is how structure and design are related and when each might be appropriate.

The Importance of Organization Structure and Design

An effective organization structure and design is one that optimizes the performance of the organization and its members by ensuring that tasks, work activities and people are organized in such a way that goals are achieved. An efficient organization structure and design is one that uses the most appropriate type and amount of resources (e.g., money, materials, people) to achieve the goals.

This means:

- organizing tasks in an efficient and effective manner to ensure work gets done with no duplication of effort
- coordinating the activities of various departments and units towards common goals
- allocating positions and people to ensure that the necessary work is done
- clarifying authority, roles and responsibilities.

But organization structure and design are not just a means of ensuring work and activities are structured and coordinated in the most efficient way, an effective structure also aids planning, decision making and minimizes work-related problems and conflict between departments and functions due to competing goals or unclear work expectations.

Whereas early classical and scientific management studies focus on finding the *one best way* of structuring an organization (e.g., Weber's bureaucracy), contingency theorists argue there is no one organization structure and design that is appropriate to every organization – instead, managers need to understand which organization structure is *most appropriate* given their organization's goals, type of technology, product or service, and the environmental demands and constraints. Managers therefore need to understand how to create an organization structure and design that takes into account all these contingencies and is both effective and efficient. To do so, they need to be able to analyse their own organization and its environment, determine the most appropriate design, implement, continually monitor and revise the structure and design to ensure it remains effective. A few OT textbooks, especially those taking a multiple perspectives approach, go further and talk about structuration theory – an approach we will discuss at the end of this chapter.

You might find it helpful to check out definitions in the Glossary, because they will help you navigate the terminology that follows.

Organization Structure: Key Concepts

Your textbook will probably describe each type of organization structure and design factor in depth. Below you will find a brief explanation of each type of structure (including goals and examples), followed by the various design factors, along with some key points to consider. Then

Table 2 on page 35 will help you make sense of the relationship between design and structure.

Functional structures

Activities and people are grouped together on the basis of similarities in work, expertise, goals or resource utilization, e.g., production, finance, sales, human resource management and engineering departments. Greenpeace International has a functional structure. If you look at the management structure on the Greenpeace International website you will see an organization chart consisting of Directors in charge of functional areas such as communications (media and images) and operations (ships and actions). This enables them to focus on key activities that help them achieve their goals.

Goals: To develop and utilize expertise in core organizational activities, and to ensure stability, continuity and minimum disruption of production or service.

These goals are exemplified in a speech by the CEO of the US railroad company, Amtrak, addressing the organization's response to a financial crisis:

> The only way to bring discipline to large organizations like Amtrak is through a tight organization, competent managers, and the budget process. My process for managing includes five basic tools:
>
> - Organization with minimum layers, individual accountability for specific functional areas, organization charts documenting the chain of command and all authorized positions;
> - Clear goals and objectives;
> - An operating budget based on monthly staffing levels;
> - A detailed multi-year capital budget; and
> - A monthly financial reporting and performance reporting for specific responsibility centers and projects.[1]

So Amtrak looked at streamlining their organization structure, particularly cutting the number of levels in the hierarchy, to reduce costs and increase direct accountability. Refer back to this example as you read through the stages of an organization's life cycle later on.

Divisional structures

The organization is split into self-contained divisions or profit centres. Each division reports to corporate headquarters, and has either its own internal functional structure (M-Form or Multi-divisional structure), or is supported by functions (HR, R & D, sales etc.) at headquarters. This will depend on the diversity of the products and the demands of the environment.

Goals: To meet the specific needs of different customer groups, to develop expertise in each product or service, to manage a diverse range of products and services more effectively and efficiently.

The organization may have its divisions based on either:

- Product or service, e.g. General Motors has a number of divisions based on the automotive brand (Saturn, Chevrolet, Hummer, etc.), and also has GMAC, a financial services division.
- Geographic region, e.g. in the US, Greyhound Bus company is organized on a geographic and a service basis including: Greyhound Canada, Greyhound Mexico, Greyhound PackageXpress, Greyhound Courier Express, Vermont Transit Company.
- Market or customer, e.g. in 1991 British Telecom announced a new organization structure that focuses on market segments including BT Retail (business and residential customers) and BT Wholesale (Corporate customers).

Matrix structures

People and activities are grouped in multi-functional teams according to the project service or contract. Teams are temporary, existing for the length of the project, and draw from different functions, for example, production, engineering, quality, marketing, finance and R & D. Each team member or project group member has two managers – a project manager (responsible for the specific project) and a functional manager. So the team member from Marketing will report to both the Marketing Manager (the functional manager) and the Project Group Manager. Raytheon, for example, have an integrated product team structure you can see on their website.

Goals: To match expertise and resources with individual customer needs and the technical and business requirements of individual projects and contracts. To adapt quickly to a dynamic environment.

So an example would be an organization working on a range of government contracts requiring in-depth technical knowledge and expertise, and the length of each contract might be five months or five years.

Other structures

Functional, divisional and matrix structures are the most common, but you also need to be aware of:

1 *Hybrid*: A mix of structures (functional, divisional, network) often used to meet the varying demands of a large diversified organization facing a range of environmental characteristics, from relatively stable to rapidly changing.

2 *Strategic alliances and joint ventures*. Both strategic alliances and joint ventures involve contractual, medium–long term relationships created between different organizations. These organizations may be competitors who want to pool resources or collaborate to challenge other competitors, or companies operating within a value or vertical chain (e.g., supplier – manufacturer – distributor). For example, in 1997, Apple and Microsoft (long time competitors) announced a five-year alliance to work on developing Macintosh compatible versions of Microsoft® Office 98, Internet Explorer 4.0 and Java technologies. This benefited Microsoft by making their products easier to use and more widely available, and Apple by increasing Macintosh products and therefore market potential. Such alliances are becoming increasingly important because they allow companies to develop technology and products by sharing costs (e.g., development, production, distribution costs) and pooling resources (e.g., expertise, knowledge, R & D, manufacturing resources). Alliances include:

- mergers and acquisitions, which are not really an alliance because one company often takes over another.
- networks (see next section).
- joint ventures, which include a separate overseeing organization. For example, the European consortium of Airbus is headquartered in France. Similarly, in the US the United Space Alliance is a joint venture established in 1995 to work on Space Shuttle programme contracts for NASA. The joint venture was initially between Lockheed Martin and Rockwell International, now Lockheed and Boeing (who bought Rockwell in 1996). The San Francisco Bay Joint Venture is a collaboration of Federal agencies, State agencies, non-profit and private organizations to 'protect, restore, increase and enhance all types of wetlands, riparian habitat and associated uplands throughout the San Francisco Bay region to benefit birds, fish and other wildlife'.[2]

Companies operating within both alliances and joint ventures help their partner organizations utilize their strengths, reduce uncertainty, learn from each other, minimize costs, share risk and facilitate low cost entry into new markets.

3 *Multinational and global.* Organizations operating in different countries:

- with headquarters in one country (multinational)
- a worldwide management team and strategy (global).

Toyota, the Japanese-headquartered motor company, has manufacturing and assembly plants in many countries including Australia, Mexico, the US, India and the UK. The company also has a number of joint venture plants, for example with General Motors in the US. Each plant operates on the 'Toyota production system', and Toyota is developing an integrated CAD/CAM system (Computer Aided Design/Computer Aided Manufacturing) so that the same database can be used throughout the world.

4 *Network and virtual organizations.* Networks of people or organizations collaborating on work or goals and often operating at a distance. These differ from strategic alliances and joint ventures because they usually involve a larger number of organizations and are concerned with operational rather than strategic issues. Functions such as manufacturing or customer service may be outsourced to contractors. Call Centres are a good example of this type of organization. A number of organizations have outsourced customer service to Call Centres located off site, some to India.

Organizational Design: Key Concepts

A useful way of thinking about these design factors is that each is a piece of a jigsaw puzzle, and all the pieces have to match for an organization structure to be effective. Managers have to balance considerations in each dimension and weigh the pros and cons of each. For example, **standardization** leads to better control because people perform according to rules and procedures and therefore it becomes easy to identify deviations. However, standardization often means new or unique situations and problems are difficult to handle, as employees are unable to use their discretion. There is also little creativity and innovation. So the design choice here is to decide what is required in a particular organization – conformity and control, or creativity? I will explain each of the design factors below and then link each to the different types of organization structure.

Differentiation

You might come across the work of Lawrence and Lorsch (1967) in your textbook, in the chapters on organizational design and on the environment. They were interested in the relationship between the environment and organization structure – in particular how the level of environmental uncertainty affects the degree of **differentiation** and the need for **integration**. We will address the two design factors here and talk about Lawrence and Lorsch's study in the section on environment and strategy.

Differentiation occurs in relation to:

- The number of levels of management (hierarchy) and how authority is assigned to the various levels in the organization, i.e., *vertical differentiation*.
- How work is divided between functions, departments and units (the division of labour), and how task responsibilities are assigned, i.e., *horizontal differentiation*.

High vertical differentiation means there are many hierarchical levels, which appear as a *tall* organization in the organization chart. High horizontal differentiation means there are many functions and departments, appearing as a *flat* organization in the organization chart.

The key is to balance vertical and horizontal differentiation so that work is carried out effectively: i.e., effort and resources are directed towards goals, there is no duplication of effort, managers can supervise work effectively and are not overburdened by too great a variety of tasks to oversee, and administrative overheads are not high.

Integration

The work has been divided (differentiated), but needs coordinating to ensure that each department, unit and level in the organization is working towards organizational goals. It is also important to ensure that the communication mechanisms necessary to achieve coordination are in place, i.e., **integration**. Integration can occur in different ways:

- Clarifying reporting relationships, responsibilities and the degree of authority at each level in the hierarchy.
- Establishing goals, rules, job descriptions and operating procedures, for each department and position.
- Creating liaison roles and positions to coordinate work across departments and functions. For example, a patient services coordinator in a hospital can liaise with various hospital departments to plan a schedule for inpatients

needing a variety of hospital services, and ensure that the departments and the patients' doctors receive the necessary information.

- Creating task forces to work on projects across departments and functions. For example, TQM or Continuous Improvement task groups are often created across departments to improve processes.
- Encourage employees to talk to employees in other departments and functions when necessary, i.e., direct contact.
- To have cross-functional teams, comprising of employees from various departments working together on a temporary or permanent basis.

The type of integration that will be most effective will depend on the product or service provided and the degree of differentiation. Managers need to balance differentiation and integration carefully to ensure the organization has a competitive advantage.

Too much integration can lead to high costs in terms of time, resources and energy expended. Too little integration can lead to high costs in terms of incomplete work, interdepartmental conflict and time spent on resolving problems.

Centralization and decentralization

This design factor addresses where decisions are made and who holds the power in the organization, but can also relate to where resources are located.

- **Centralization**: when decisions are made at the top of the organization by a CEO or a senior management team. Other employees in the organization have little input into the decision-making process and often follow instructions. Resources are located at headquarters or a single site. For example, an organization might have one centralized warehouse that supplies materials and equipment to factories located throughout the country.
- **Decentralization**: when decisions are made at all levels in the hierarchy by those who have the expertise. Resources are situated at various locations.

Centralization can ensure decisions are based on organizational goals, greater control and cost effectiveness in terms of resources. However, the downsides of centralization are that employee expertise and knowledge are under-utilized, decision making can be lengthy as problems are referred up the hierarchy, and local needs are ignored. While many organizations still operate in a centralized manner, the move towards job enrichment through self-directed teams and greater individual autonomy has led to greater decentralization. Decentralization can lead to greater creativity, innovation, flexibility and motivation, as people with expertise respond to problems and the need for improvements.

Standardization and mutual adjustment

Should employees conform to rules and follow specific operating processes and work procedures, or use their individual judgement and initiative in their work? To clarify, standardization does *not* refer to producing a standardized product or service, but to the procedures governing *how* that product or service is made. **Standardization** is a way of ensuring that people carry out their work in the same way. This will depend on organizational goals; the nature of the work, product or service; and the management style. Many government organizations operate through standardization. Imagine if you and your sister went to the Driver and Vehicle Licensing Agency (or the DMV in the US) for a driver's licence; you didn't get your licence but your sister did because the issuing officer felt she did a much better job of explaining why she needed one! In this case, the lack of standardized rules for issuing licences and of a standardized application process leads to unfair and inconsistent decision making. Standardization remedies this and also allows the organization to deal with a large number of customers in a timely and efficient way. **Mutual adjustment** means employees can use their discretion in doing their work.

Formalization

Formalization refers to the degree to which the organization has written, formal and well-defined organization charts, job descriptions, operating procedures, rules, policies, and requires formal written communication – versus informal and less defined ways of working and interacting. Managers may want to encourage less formal ways of relating, especially if the organization needs to be flexible and responsive to changing environmental demands.

Mechanistic and organic structures (Burns and Stalker, 1966)

Burns and Stalker linked structure and design to the type of environment in which the organization operates. They suggested that in stable, predictable environments, *mechanistic* structures are most appropriate. These are structures with:

- High horizontal and vertical differentiation.
- High degree of formalization.
- Centralized decision making.

- Standardization.
- Close supervision with authority and status based on position.

In changing unpredictable and dynamic environments, *organic* structures are more appropriate:

- High/complex horizontal and vertical integration.
- Low formalization.
- Decentralized decision making.
- **Mutual adjustment.**
- Personal expertise, creativity without supervision.

Note here the term 'appropriate'.... this should be raising flags that Burns and Stalker took a contingency approach! You might also connect mechanistic structures with bureaucracies and many functional organizations, and organic structures with matrix organizations.

Table 2 summarizes the main types of organization structure, how the design factors tend to play out in each type, and when each type of structure is most appropriate.

It is important to remember that these are general guidelines, each organization differs, so that within a functional structure there may be design variations. To give you an illustration, the Ritz Carlton Hotel has a functional structure, with high horizontal differentiation, specialization and formalization. However, it operates in a more decentralized way with employee work teams, decision making by employees at all levels, and self-directed work teams working on quality improvement projects. So as you are looking at the organization charts of various companies, you may see a combination of structures, for example, divisional and functional. Also remember that the organization chart doesn't give you a complete picture of the way the organization functions – organizational culture also plays an important role.

Some General Guidelines for Organizational Design

As I mentioned earlier, *the efficiency and effectiveness of the organization depends on making sure these design factors fit together.* Although there are no hard and fast rules or ideal models of organizing, and there will be variations within particular organizations, some general guidelines are as follows.

If you are manufacturing a standard product (e.g., burgers, chocolate bars, steel pipes) or providing a standardized service, where the product/service rarely changes and needs to be consistent, and you are producing a

Table 2   Organization structure and design

Structure	Design factors	Useful when
Functional Activities and people are grouped together on the basis of similarities in work, expertise, goals or resource utilization.	*Vertical differentiation:* often high. *Horizontal differentiation:* often high. *Integration:* clear reporting relationships, goals, procedures, task forces. *Specialization:* highly specialized. *De/Centralization:* Tend to be more centralized. *Standardization:* rules, operating procedures, equipment, resources etc. *Formalization:* often highly formalized.	The organization has one, or a small range of, products or services. The goal is to produce large quantities at relatively low cost. Efficiency is a key factor.
Divisional (M-Form) Self-contained business units, which often contain their own functional departments.	*Vertical differentiation:* often high. *Horizontal differentiation:* often high. *Integration:* clear reporting relationships, goals, procedures, task forces. *Specialization:* highly specialized within divisions. *De/Centralization:* Tends to be decentralized to each division, but often centralized within divisions. *Standardization:* rules, operating procedures, equipment, resources etc. within each division. *Formalization:* often highly formalized.	The organization has a number of different products or services. Each product or service has different requirements. The organization needs to respond to different environmental or regional demands.
Matrix	*Vertical differentiation:* often low. *Horizontal differentiation:* often high. *Integration:* direct contact and cross functional teams. *Specialization:* highly specialized but able to be generalists in understanding project demands. *De/Centralization:* Decentralized, problems resolved and decisions made by groups. *Mutual adjustment:* initiative and discretion in deciding how to achieve project goals. *Formalization:* often low formalization, flexible to meet changing product or contract requirements.	The organization works on a range of individual customer contracts or projects, each with different specifications. There is a need to develop project-based technical knowledge and expertise.

large quantity or dealing with many customers who have the same needs, then a centralized, standardized and formalized design is likely to be more effective because it gives greater control over the product and service, and you are less likely to encounter variations. You can also maintain lower costs in this way. Government organizations, health care organizations, the postal service and food manufacturers are good examples of organizations where this design best works. Hospitals and food manufacturers also need to maintain strict standards of quality and hygiene.

If your organization provides a more individualized service, or products based on individual customer needs, then a more decentralized, mutual adjustment, informal structure would be appropriate because the organization needs to be flexible in assessing and responding to individual customer requirements, for example, software design companies who customize products to individual customer needs.

Sometimes, more hybrid forms of organizational design are required. One example I am familiar with involves an initiative headed by a County Court and County Health system. The Court system had identified a number of strategic goals, including:

- Increasing access to the community
- Streamlining administrative systems
- Increasing customer responsiveness
- Improving the quality of service.

In the past, domestic violence incidents and the resulting family mediation services were dealt with by a number of separate agencies: the Department of Health and Human Services, the District Attorney's Office, Probation Services and the Superior Court. Families had to visit all the agencies, each located in separate buildings. In order to streamline family support mediation services and make the system more responsive to client needs, a new one-stop Information Center was created. Representatives from each agency were located in one building, which meant they could collaborate on a face-to-face basis in providing all the necessary services for their clients. So in this case each Agency had it's own internal functional structure, with standardized rules and procedures, but recognized that the old bureaucratic system resulted in failure to comply with requirements, and families failing to receive the necessary support because the system was so complex to navigate. While the internal functional structure still existed, the new initiative was based on a more matrix-oriented structure to improve collaboration and focus on client needs.

Contemporary Approaches to Organization Structure and Design

More critically oriented and multiple perspectives-based OT textbooks will incorporate additional perspectives on organization structure. It's impossible to cover all the different approaches here, but among them you might find a discussion of *structuration* theory, feminist approaches to organization and flexible **specialization**. Each offers a different way of thinking about organization structure and design. For example, structuration theorists see structure emerging in the routine behaviours of people, and then influencing those behaviours. Feminist organizational theorists suggest that many organization structures are gender-biased, and that we need to consider alternative and more inclusive structures.

Structuration theory

Routines have long been regarded as a factor of organizational life in the sense of standard operating procedures or technical routines associated with the use of equipment. Such routines are mechanisms for preserving and transferring knowledge and skills, for coordinating activity and accomplishing work. However, some contemporary organization theorists move away from the idea that routines are *things,* suggesting instead they are repeated behaviours and patterns of relationships created in the everyday interactions of people. For instance, a boss may regularly ask a member of staff for certain information and this type of exchange will become a routine or stable feature of their relationship. Similarly, an employee might find that she needs to work regularly with someone from another department who has a specialized area of expertise critical to part of her work. As these routines become habit, they become taken for granted as part of work and structure. So the routines we create, we eventually see as existing apart from us and maybe even constraining our action. How many times do you hear people say 'that's the system', or 'that's the way it's always been done'? Anthony Giddens describes this process in which our actions create structure and then the 'structure' constrains our actions, as *structuration* theory.

Other organization theorists have taken this further and view organization structure as always emerging in the routines and *improvisations* of its members. Karl Weick and Mary Jo Hatch for example, use the jazz metaphor as a way of explaining this process, and you can find their articles listed at the end of this section. This offers an interesting alternative to traditional ways of thinking about structure.

Feminist approaches to organizing

A number of *feminist* scholars argue that bureaucratic forms of organization are male-gendered and male-dominated. Bureaucracies privilege and justify hierarchy by claiming that power, position, evaluations and promotions, etc. are based on 'rational' criteria associated with technical competence. The definitions of 'rationality' are male-gendered constructions (objective, competitive, individual performance, impersonality, etc.) made by one group of people that can result in the domination of other minority groups. This reinforces white male-gendered culture and practices. Feminist organizations use flexible and cooperative designs.

Flexible specialization

Postmodern approaches to organizing are sometimes associated with post-Fordism and flexible specialization. Whereas Fordism embraces mass production and modernist principles of organization – standardization, specialization, the division of labour, tight control and the functional nature of products – post-Fordism focuses on flexible and flatter organization structures, niche markets, a skilled workforce, innovation and 'lifestyle' consumption – a radical restructuring of ways of organizing, doing business and employing people. Michael Piore and Charles Sabel (1984) coined the term *flexible specialization* to describe these characteristics. They argued that a demand for more customized products and services, rapid technological change, and increasing market differentiation led to the need for organizations to combine the economies of scale associated with mass production with a flexible use of production and labour. The characteristics of flexible specialization include:

- Short product life cycles and continual product and service innovation
- Monitoring consumer habits as the basis for adjusting production
- The production of high quality products through total quality control
- Versatility – the continual reconfiguration of technology and resources
- Decentralized decision making and an equitable distribution of knowledge amongst all organizational employees
- Trust-based relationships
- Branding is important – sign value over use value.

These characteristics are often seen as best enacted through the collaboration of mainly small specialized organizations rather than any single organization.

INTEGRATIVE CASE

Let's go back to the restaurant example on page 5, and look at some of the design choices you might face as the owner. Remember:

> You own and manage a restaurant in your local town, which can seat up to 80 people, and is open for lunch and dinner. You serve an international cuisine, the price range of an entrée is moderate to high, and you offer elegant décor and a romantic atmosphere. You employ a staff of 30 people, which includes an Assistant Manager, chef and cooks, bar staff, waitpersons, cleaners, cashier...

So your design choices might be as follows.

1 *Differentiation and integration:*

- Low vertical differentiation with three levels in the hierarchy. Too many levels (e.g., employing an additional person to supervise the waitstaff and report to the Assistant Manager) means you would be distant from your employees and the customer, and it would be costly.
- Fairly high horizontal differentiation with five different functions – but on the upside your organization is small enough to allow people to communicate easily on a face-to-face basis.
- Integration through direct contact because employees need to talk to each other directly to coordinate customer orders and ensure they are met in a timely manner.
- As you can see by the dotted triangle, a *flat* organization:

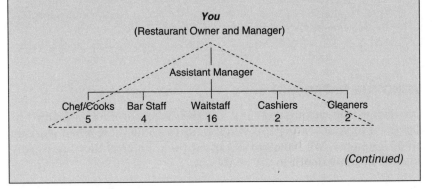

You
(Restaurant Owner and Manager)

Assistant Manager

Chef/Cooks	Bar Staff	Waitstaff	Cashiers	Gleaners
5	4	16	2	2

(Continued)

(Continued)

2 ***Centralization:*** Because you are a small owner-operated organiza-tion where excellent service, a fine dining experience, and cost effectiveness are key goals, centralized decision making is probably more appropriate. As the owner, although you might delegate the day-to-day operations to your Assistant Manager, you will probably want control over ordering food and equipment, oversight over work sched-uling and customer satisfaction, as well as making key decisions. This means you can also utilize your knowledge and expertise, ensure your goals are being met, and make decisions quickly. In larger organiza-tions, as you might imagine, centralization can overburden a CEO or senior managers with too many decisions, which might lead to longer response times on problems.

3 ***Standardization:*** Standardization will be important in maintaining cost-effectiveness, hygiene standards, and customer satisfaction for a timely, reliable and high quality dining experience. You might require standardization in relation to cooking and cleaning proce-dures, equipment, portion control, food quality, dress of waitstaff and bar staff, and particular ways of interacting with customers to ensure consistent service.

4 ***Formalization:*** Smaller organizations tend to be less formalized than larger ones, because control and integration can occur through direct communication. You might have formal written job descriptions for each position, so that employees are clear about what needs to be done, but you are probably not going to have formal oper-ating procedures because these will be time consuming to write and you can convey information and instructions face-to-face.

As the owner of the restaurant, knowledge of organization structure and design could help you make some key decisions on how to organize and what might be appropriate. It can help you be more proactive in terms of anticipating what needs to be done – and what doesn't – rather than react-ing to problems as they arise.

USING THE MATERIAL

Do review the advantages and disadvantages of each structure as described in your textbook as you'll need to know these when working on assignments. We have not discussed them here, as they are usually covered in some depth in OT textbooks.

1 Organization structures should not be carved in stone.' Discuss, giving examples to support your points.

When answering this question you do not need to describe each type of structure, but think about why managers might need to redesign their organization's structure. This really requires an overview of organization structure and design. If you've discussed environment and strategy, then you will see that structure changes through the life cycle of an organization, and that as environmental demands change, so will the appropriateness of an organization's structure (e.g. Burns and Stalker). Also consider environmental changes (increased customer responsiveness), changes in business strategy (e.g. product diversification, new geographical markets, retrenchment), organizations grow and go through life cycles, increased competition might result in joint ventures, and so on. Think about how these factors might influence organization structure and design and give examples of how these might change – or how organizations have changed in response.

2 Why do managers need to understand organization structure and design? Give examples to support your reasoning.

Of course the simple answer is that managers need to make sure that the organization structure and design optimizes productivity and performance and supports the achievement of organizational goals and the implementation of business strategy. But you need to say more! Give examples of how it does so, and how inappropriate design can lead to problems. Review the points in the Integrative Case and the Importance of Organization Structure and Design section.

3 What are the advantages and disadvantages of a functional (divisional or matrix) structure?

This is a straightforward question and usually the material is presented in your OT textbook. Rather than just reproducing a list of advantages and disadvantages of a particular structure, give reasons why and also provide examples. You can find examples in your textbook and on the Internet.

You might also be asked to analyse the appropriateness of organization structure and design factors in a case study, in an organization with which you are familiar, or an organization you find on the Internet.

Taking it **FURTHER**

Organizations are facing increasingly complex issues, for example, how to balance the costs and benefits of a multinational company, how to integrate and control divisions, how to manage outsourced activities, how to coordinate work in strategic alliances or joint ventures, and so on. There is rarely a simple answer. Organizational design often means balancing considerations, and organizations are rarely the pure structures (functional, divisional, etc.) identified in your textbook. Many companies will have a number of characteristics relating to a particular structure, but also some differences because they have adapted to their particular circumstances. So how then might you use this material? How might structuration theory or feminist ways of organizing help you structure and design organizations in more effective and equitable ways?

Notes

1 http://www.amtrak.com/servlet/ContentServer?pagename=Amtrak/ am2Copy/Simple_Copy_Page&cid=1081442674405&c=am2Copy&ssid= 172, accessed January 2007.

2 http://www.sfbayjv.org/ (San Francisco Bay Joint Venture), accessed January 2007.

Textbook Guide

CHILD: *Chapters 2, 3, 4, 9, 10 and 16.*
DAFT: *Chapters 3, 5 and 6.*
HATCH WITH CUNLIFFE: *Chapters 4 and 9.*
JONES: *Chapters 4, 5 and 6.*
WATSON: *Chapters 2 and 7.*

Additional Reading

For alternative ideas on organization structure, you might want to read:

Ashcraft, K. L. (2001) 'Organized dissonance: feminist bureaucracy as hybrid form', *Academy of Management Journal*, 44/6: 1301–22.

Hatch, M. J. (1993) 'The empty spaces of organizing: how improvisational jazz helps redescribe organizational structure', *Organization Studies*, 20: 75–100.

Mintzberg, H. and Vander Heyden, L. (1999) 'Organigraphs: drawing how companies really work', *Harvard Business Review*, 77: 87–95 (they present an alternative way of charting structure and design).

Weick, Karl (1998) 'Improvisation as a mindset for organizational analysis', *Organization Science*, 9: 543–55 (a special issue on jazz and improvisation).

2	
technology	

When we think of technology today, it's often computer technology that comes to mind, yet the study of technology goes back over 40 years. During that time, organization theorists have been interested in how different types of technology impact organization structure and design. Early studies focused on manufacturing and service technologies, while the last 20 years have seen an emergence of work on new technologies (computers, microelectronics, etc.).

Technology is important because it has an impact on organizational performance in a number of ways. Successful performance and maintaining company competitiveness depends on:

- using up-to-date technology to improve efficiency, productivity, service, quality and innovation
- aligning technology, organizational design and organizational strategy.

So we'll begin with some key definitions of technology, then summarize the three main ways of classifying technology (*typologies*), look at key developments in new technology, and then discuss the relationship between technology and organizational design.

Definitions of Technology

Technology refers to the equipment, work processes, techniques, knowledge, skills and activities used to convert raw materials to the finished product – or from a systems perspective, the means by which inputs are transformed into outputs. Every organization utilizes some form of technology, whether it's a manufacturing plant, a software company, a hospital or a university. Technology is also used at different levels: the organizational (input → transformation process → output), departmental/unit/function (an Accident & Emergency Department, a Public Relations Department), and individual (expertise) levels.

You might also come across the following terms:

- Core technology – the technology (transformation process) used specifically to produce the product or service. For example, the core technology in McDonald's includes preparation and food assembly (cutting, cooking, making

the salads, burgers, etc.), the equipment (grills, knives, cash registers) and serving the customer.
- Non-core technology – technology used that is not directly related to the product or service. For example, at McDonald's this includes Accounting, Media Relations and Human Resource Management functions.
- The technological imperative – the idea that technology determines an organization's structure and design.
- Typology – a classification of different types, in this case of different types of technology.

Typologies of Technology: Key Concepts

The *technological imperative* is evident in the work of three influential studies of technology done by Joan Woodward (1965) James Thompson (1967) and Charles Perrow (1967). Each classifies different types of technology (*typology*), and examines how the type of technology influences organization structure. However, each takes a different perspective:

- Joan Woodward argues that technical complexity (the extent to which the manufacturing process is mechanized) affects structure.
- James Thompson argues that technological interdependence affects structure.
- Charles Perrow argues that task variability and analysability affect structure.

The value of using all three typologies to analyse the relationship between technology and structure is that they offer different perspectives, and therefore a more complete analysis. I will summarize the main elements of each typology and then we will use them to analyse technology in our restaurant.

Joan Woodward, *Industrial Organization* (1965)

Joan Woodward's study of 100 firms in south-east Essex is regarded as a classic in OT. She focused on core technology at the organizational level, and demonstrated that commercially successful companies organized themselves in a manner compatible with their technology. The degree of *technical complexity* – or mechanization – was a determining factor of structure (see Table 3).

Table 3 Woodward's Typology of Technology (1965)

Technical complexity	Type of technology	Implications for structure
Low	Unit/small batch – products made to customer order, e.g., wine, electronics.	Flat hierarchy, low centralization and formalization. Organic.
↓	Large batch. Mass production. Defined tasks, e.g., cars, paper bags.	Wide span, centralized and formalized. Mechanistic.
High	Continuous process Flow of product, e.g., oil, beer.	Tall. Low centralization and formalization. Organic.

James Thompson, *Organizations in Action* (1967)

Thompson suggested the type and degree of *technological interdependence* affects organization structure, and he identified three different types of interdependence (see Table 4 overleaf).

Let's take an example of each type of technology and the related type of interdependence to illustrate the connections:

Mediating technology and pooled interdependence can be seen in a Doctor's practice, as individual physicians work independently and coordinate a number of services for their patients. Each Doctor has their own patients, but the practice has a common medical records system, and a common referral system to local hospitals and other services (*pooled interdependence*). Your Doctor may 'mediate' between you and hospital services such as physical therapy, outpatient testing or inpatient treatment. In this situation, there are routine procedures every Doctor has to follow for referral and treatment. Computer technology allows Doctors to manage their case load and schedule patient hospital visits – so work is coordinated through routine procedures and technology.

Long-linked technology and *sequential interdependence* may be seen in assembly lines and continuous process technology where the outputs of one person or department are the inputs of another. The manufacture of chocolate bars is a good example. The process begins at the factory with the cleaning of the cocoa beans, followed by the blending and

Table 4   Thompson's Typology of Task Interdependence (1967)

Type of technology	Type of interdependence	Coordination
Mediating technology The inputs, work and outputs of each department or person are solely their own, e.g. Banks, supermarkets, Doctor's practices.	**Pooled interdependence** Each person works independently towards organizational goals.	Observable uniform standards, routine procedures, rules, SOPs, electronic systems, computer technology.
Long-linked technology Outputs of one department/person are inputs for another, e.g., assembly lines, process technologies.	**Sequential interdependence** The work of one person/department depends on the work of the previous person down the line.	Planning, standardized procedures, routinization, control.
Intensive technology The inputs, work and outputs of people/departments interrelate, e.g. hospital emergency departments, film/TV industry.	**Reciprocal interdependence** The activities of different people are interdependent in order to achieve goals.	Mutual adjustment, flexibility, interaction, liaison.

Reprinted with thanks to the Estate of James David Thompson.

roasting of beans from different countries. A hulling machine separates the bean from its shell, and the beans are milled (ground) into a liquid. The next stage involves the mixing of the chocolate liquid with sugar and milk, which is then dried into chocolate crumb powder. Cocoa butter is then added to form a paste, which is smoothed out, poured into moulds, cooled and wrapped. You can see a video of this process at http://www.hersheys.com/discover/tour_video.asp.

Intensive technology and *reciprocal interdependence* occurs when people and/or departments have to work together to achieve goals – an Accident and Emergency Department in a hospital is a good example. Various personnel are involved in the treatment of casualties, and this can include: ambulance personnel, surgeons, physicians, triage nurses, administration, anesthesiologists, medical technicians, lab technicians, and so on. A & E Departments have to deal with a wide range of patients and conditions, little planning can be done in advance so personnel have to be flexible, responsive to specific patient conditions, and interact with each other as and when needed.

So in summary, as you might imagine, intensive technology requires a more organic structure to be able to deal with all the different types of work, equipment and interactions required to meet the goal. Long-linked or mediating technology requires a more mechanistic structure because work is more routine, structured, and controllable.

Charles Perrow, *Organizational Analysis* (1970)

Perrow studied mainly non-core technology at the department level, suggesting that departments need to be structured around the technology they use. For Perrow, technological complexity relates to whether tasks are routine or non-routine, and this depends on two dimensions:

- *Task variability:* whether work involves a large number of unique and unexpected situations and problems. If 'yes' there are a large number of different problems = high variety, which means more complexity. If 'no', routine work and problems = low variety and little complexity.
- *Task analysability:* whether the work process can be analysed and broken down into routine steps, whether standard procedures can be applied to problem solving, and whether techniques and instruction manuals can be developed. If 'yes' work can be analysed = high analysability and low complexity. If 'no' work cannot be analysed, tasks and problem solving depend on experience = low analysability and high complexity.

These two factors help categorize the type of technology and therefore the type of structure that is most appropriate (see Table 5 overleaf).

If you think about your work, or perhaps a job you've had in the past, you might be able to identify its variability and analysability and fit it into one of Perrow's four types. If you are a clerical officer in a Bank or a customer service employee in a department store then the technology is probably *routine*, a car mechanic falls into *engineering* technology, management consulting perhaps into *craft* technology, and a biotech researcher into *non-routine* technology.

If we take this further and look at the impact of the type of technology on structure, Perrow says that *routine technology* often leads to: a tall hierarchy, standardization, specialization, formalization and centralized decision making. In other words a more mechanistic organization structure. On the otherhand, *non-routine* technology often leads to a

Table 5   Perrow's Typology of Technology (1967)

	Low	High
		Task variability	

Low	***CRAFT***: few unique situations, and few procedures for dealing with them because can depend on experience and intuition, e.g., furniture making, jewelry design.	***NON-ROUTINE***: many new and unique tasks and no routine ways of dealing with these, e.g., medical research, software design.
Task analysability		
High	***ROUTINE***: standard work, few unexpected situations, with known procedures for dealing with them, e.g., assembly line, clerical.	***ENGINEERING***: a variety of situations that are dealt with through known techniques and procedures, e.g., engineering, accounting, architectural design firms.

Reprinted by permission of the ASA and the author.

flatter hierarchy characterized by mutual adjustment, low formalization and decentralized decision making, that is, a more organic organization structure.

Contemporary Approaches to Technology

In addition to the issues above, if your textbook takes a more critical or multiple perspectives approach, you might also encounter the following theories in relation to the study of technology.

Structuration theory

I outlined Gidden's structuration theory in the first section of this Part – the idea that people create structures or routines that then influence their behaviour. The theories discussed up to this point have assumed that technology is some *thing* that determines organization structure and human actions, i.e., the *technological imperative*. A number of organization theorists and sociologists take a structuration approach to suggest that technology takes on meaning as people and technology interact. In other words, the meaning and use of old and new forms of technology continually emerge in the interactions and interpretations of people using the technology. This might make more sense if you think about your computer or laptop. Not everyone uses their laptop for the same purpose or in exactly the same way. I write papers, lectures, create powerpoint slides, and play the occasional game on mine. My daughter writes essays, instant messages, plays DVDs, and listens to music on hers. A friend uses his for graphic design and artwork. You might use your laptop for other purposes. The point is, that we shape the use of technology – just as technology influences what we do. We improvise and use it in creative and unique ways, we develop particular routines around its use, and in doing so we give technology meaning. Wanda Orlikowski (2000) coined the term *technologies-in-practice* to describe this process of routine and improvisation. You will find her article listed in the Additional Reading at the end of this section. Look around you at work, school or home and think about how people create and are influenced by technologies-in-practice.

Actor-network theory

Actor-network theory (ANT) is a way of viewing and studying organizations as continually shifting networks of human and non-human materials. These materials change and mingle to form different modes of ordering (ways of organizing), which are the recurring patterns generated and performed in interaction. John Law, a British sociologist, used actor-network theory to study a UK Laboratory. Law suggests that although we see organizations as entities (departments, information systems, etc.), they are heterogeneous networks in which rankings and order emerge. For example, people are ranked in interactions according to whether others need their expertise, whether they are creative or perform routine activities, whether they are workaholics, their place in administrative orderings (their position), and their ability to interact with sophisticated or less sophisticated physical materials and equipment. These interactions carry 'scripts', embedded routines that constrain and enable activity (remember structuration theory). For example, a computer and its software carry scripts for the type of physical movements required to use it, for what we can do with it, and for who can use it. Rankings occur as some individuals may be more expert than others in enacting these scripts. Actor-network theorists study technology and organization structure (which they define as the process of organizing) by examining how all the various elements of the network (people, technology, actions, knowledge, documents, buildings, etc.) come together to create and sustain network stabilities; how technical objects and work processes change through the interactions of network materials; and how certain configurations might lead to network inefficiencies.

New Technology, Information Technology and Advanced Manufacturing Technology

Most OT textbooks have a chapter on new technology because it has had a major impact on the way organizations do business and organize work and resources. E-commerce is a good example: you may have ordered your OT textbook from Amazon, bought your customized personal computer from Dell, ordered your groceries online and had them delivered to your door... So technology has not only impacted large corporations, but our personal lives and also small crafts and home businesses. For example, you can buy individually designed, handcrafted jewelry made by an artist in the desert in New Mexico, and have it shipped to your home in the UK. Previously, the artist would have depended on passing trade or on travelling to various craft fairs.

Your textbook will probably discuss the various forms of new technology, including **information technology**, **advanced manufacturing technology** and **management information systems**. If you are unfamiliar with new technology, this can get confusing – check the Glossary for simple definitions! Let's look at how new technology might impact organization structure and design. Karl Weick (1990), who takes a social constructionist perspective on organization theory, offers a different way of thinking about new technologies, suggesting they are characterized by abstract, continuous and stochastic events. Take online airfare reservations as an example. When going on holiday, you can book your trip online any month, any day, any time during the day or night (continuous events), unless, of course, unexpectedly the system is down for some unknown reason that has to be figured out (a stochastic event). In fixing the problem, the tech people have to probably use trial and error to figure out what the problem is, because the system is complex and they cannot actually see the work process – the data flow, moving parts, the linkages between the hardware, software, the Internet service provider and the Internet itself (abstract events). Weick suggests that new technology involves more mental rather than physical processes and is open to many different interpretations – *equivoque*. You can find a reference to his work in the Additional Reading at the end of this section. You might also want to check out the website for the UK's DTI Manufacturing Advisory Service which has a number of useful resources on manufacturing technology – including advanced manufacturing technology.

The impact of new technology on organization structure and design

In general, we can summarize the impact of new technologies as having reduced the need for:

- physical proximity – of organizations to customers and employees to each other and their manager
- hierarchical controls
- direct integrating mechanisms – supervision, liaison roles, face-to-face task groups, etc., because integration can take place through electronic linking.

New technologies can also lead to:

- the creation of virtual and **network** organizations and teams
- greater decentralization of decision making because data is more readily available to all levels of employees
- increased spans of control and decreased hierarchical levels (flatter organizations) as managers supervise employees who deal with larger amounts of information and software programmes correct errors and make the exchange of information easier and faster.
- based on Weick's notion of equivoque, a more organic structure in order to deal with unexpected, complex and unprogrammed problems.

INTEGRATIVE CASE

Let's look at our restaurant example to pull all these concepts together:

Your restaurant seats up to 80 people, is open for lunch and dinner, and serves an international cuisine. You employ a staff of 30 people, including an Assistant Manager, chef and cooks, bar staff, waitpersons, cleaners, and a cashier.

1 *Core technology*: The process of preparing, cooking and serving the food to customers.

2 *Levels of technology*: *Organization* level – inputs (vegetables, meat, wine, etc.) → conversion process (food preparation, cooking, etc.) → outputs (serving meals, drinks); *Function* level – e.g., cooking involves preparation and cooking utensils and equipment, ovens, grills and knowledge of food, recipes, cooking techniques, hygiene, etc.; *Individual* level – e.g., a bar person's knowledge of alcohol, types of drinks and how to mix them, customer service, etc.

(Continued)

(Continued)

3 *Technical complexity*: Using Woodward's typology, you will fall under small batch production – providing a range of meals for lunch and dinner menus. The choice and number of each dish served each day will vary according to customer preference.

4 *Interdependence*: Using Thompson's typology, your restaurant will probably rely on intensive technology and reciprocal interdependence. Although waitstaff will take orders to pass on to the cooks and bar staff, the work process will be unique to each customer's needs. Compare this to McDonald's where a limited range of food is prepared in advance and stocked ready for the customer (long-linked, sequential).

5 *Task complexity*: Under Perrow's typology at the department level – for waitstaff, task variability is low because you have menus and customers are not going to choose anything unexpected. The tasks are also analysable in terms of ordering, serving and customer service. Your chef and cooks will also have fairly low variability and analysability – even though you have a range of dishes and your menu might change, there are specific recipes and cooking techniques. So unless your Chef wants to be really creative, you will probably fall into the routine type of technology!

This example shows why it's important to utilize different typologies, because each gives a different perspective. Using Woodward's small batch and Thompson's intensive technology and reciprocal interdependence, you would need a fairly flat, flexible, organic organization. Using Perrow's routine technology, some degree of formalization and standardization are required, for example, in terms of ordering supplies, auditing, hygiene and health standards, and cash management.

You may be using new technology to order supplies or market your restaurant, but as it's not your core technology, do you think it will influence structure? How might you use structuration theory to think differently about your restaurant's technology?

USING THE MATERIAL

Don't just think about technology in a manufacturing sense – remember that service organizations also utilize technology in the form of equipment, new technologies and work processes. If you work for local government, McDonald's, ASDA, a transportation organization or a local doctor, you can still apply the theories and ideas from this chapter. You should also be getting a sense of how all the various OT topics interrelate. In this case, technology affects structure.

You will probably be given questions on the relationship between technology and organization structure, for example:

1 Discuss how technology impacts organization structure and design.

You might want to begin your essay by saying the question draws on the idea of the technological imperative, and explain why the question is important (see this section's introduction). You will need to review the impact of both traditional and new technologies in this question. I have summarized the latter for you already. In relation to more traditional manufacturing technologies you will need to cite the work of Woodward, Thompson and Perrow and give examples. This does not mean describing each theory, but pulling out the essential points of each typology. For example, 'The type of technology varies in each organization according to its complexity (Woodward, 1965), whether tasks are routine or non-routine (Perrow, 1967), and the degree of interdependence involved in the work process (Thompson, 1967)'. Give examples of each, e.g., an organization manufacturing chocolate would be an example of long-linked technology (Thompson, 1967), and in this case a functional structure is more appropriate because of the need to produce a large quantity of a product... (see Tables 2 and 3 for further information).

2 How do new and advanced technologies impact organization structure and design?

Expand on the summary provided in this section and give examples.

3 You may be asked to analyse a case study, which means identifying the types of technologies used, how these relate to structure, and whether problems exist because structure doesn't fit the type of technology.

The Integrative Case offers an example of how you can analyse a case study. You would then go on to identify problems and how a mismatch between the complexity (Woodward), interdependence (Thompson) and routineness (Perrow) of the technology and the appropriate structure and design factors identified in these studies might contribute to those problems.

Taking it **FURTHER**

Cyborganization

Remember films such as *Blade Runner*, *The Terminator* and *Star Trek's* Borg, and the idea of social and genetic engineering and the hybrid human-machine: the cyborg? While this offers dark images of fractured identities, exploitation and domination – think of cyborganization as the exploration of the relationship between high-technology, the body, organizations, and our social and organizational life. This is a complex subject, but if you are interested, have a look at the work of Donna Haraway (1991; 1997), and Martin Parker and Robert Cooper (1998). They offer a postmodern perspective on technology.

Textbook Guide

DAFT: *Chapters 7 and 8.*
HATCH WITH CUNLIFFE: *Chapter 5.*
JONES: *Chapter 9.*

Additional Reading

Haraway, D. J. (1991) *Simians, Cyborgs and Women: The Reinvention of Nature.* New York: Routledge.

Haraway, D. J. (1997) *Modest-Witness@Second-Millenium.FemaleMan-Meets-Oncomouse: Feminism and Technoscience.* New York and London: Routledge.

Law, J. (ed.) (1991) *A Sociology of Monsters: Essays on Power, Technology and Domination.* London: Routledge (social constructionist and actor network theory studies of technology).

Law, J. (1994) *Organizing Modernity.* Oxford: Blackwell.

Orlikowski, W. J. (2000) 'Using technology and constituting structures: a practice lens for studying technology in organization', *Organization Science,* 11: 404–28.

Orr, J. E. (1996) *Talking About Machines: An Ethnography of a Modern Job.* ILR Press: Cornell University Press (an interesting study of Xerox technicians and the relationship between technology, social practices, structure and organizational culture).

Parker, M. and Cooper, R. (1998) 'Cyborganization: cinema as nervous system', in J. Hassard and R. Holliday, *Organization Representation: Work and Organizations in Popular Culture*. London: Sage. pp. 201–28.

Weick, K. E. (1990) 'Technology as equivoque: sensemaking in new technologies', in Paul S. Goodman, Lee S. Sproull and Associates (eds), *Technology and Organizations*. San Francisco: Jossey-Bass. pp. 1–44.

Zuboff, S. (1988) *In the Age of the Smart Machine: The Future of Work and Power*. New York: Basic Books.

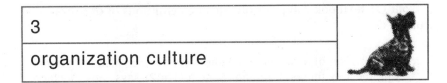

3

organization culture

Organization culture can be a difficult topic to grasp because culture is not something tangible, is expressed in many ways, and has a major influence on how employees behave, do their jobs, and interact with people both inside and outside the organization. You experience organizational culture everyday at work, yet probably don't think about it because it's a taken-for-granted part of organizational life. Think of culture as the personality of the organization: the values, beliefs and the way employees act, etc. This chapter is organized differently. Rather than picking out key theories as in other chapters, we will look at key issues, because it makes more sense given that culture is less theoretical and more about organizational stories, language and values. We will begin by defining culture and why it's important, look at the various influences on organizational culture, explore in more depth what organizational culture is, and then look at the relationship between culture and ethical behaviour.

What is Organization Culture?

Culture has long been a topic of study within the social sciences, and we probably all have an image of anthropologists studying distant primitive societies to uncover their customs, traditions and practices. While this might seem a far cry from organizational life (although maybe sometimes not quite so far removed!), organization culture scholars examine similar issues. Many use *ethnographic* methods – spending time 'living' in the organization, observing meetings, interviewing employees, discussing issues, etc. to try to identify common assumptions, values and practices that influence the way things are done in an organization. Note that this is an example of work within Burrell and Morgan's (1979) interpretivist paradigm. So what aspects of organization culture would ethnographers be studying and why? Will they be just observing and collecting data, or asking organizational members about various experiences and meanings?

Your OT textbook will probably include definitions of organizational culture as:

1 The basic set of assumptions, beliefs or accepted meanings underlying the way things are done. Schein (1992) says these include: what is real, what is right, how time is viewed (as money, to be invested in carefully to benefit the future), how we should relate to others, how we view personal and shared space, and assumptions about people and whether they are self-motivated. These can be very powerful because they are taken for granted as being normal, they weave through our actions, and we usually do not question them. They influence what we see as being right or wrong.

2 The values underlying actions and decisions. Some OT textbooks differentiate between *terminal values* (outcomes such as increased profitability, social responsibility) and *instrumental values* (desired behaviours such as competitiveness, collaboration). Many organizations now list their core values as a means of highlighting to employees what is important. For example, Ben and Jerry's Ice Cream identify their values as:

- We strive to create economic opportunities for those who have been denied them and to advance new models of economic justice that are sustainable and replicable.
- We strive to minimize our negative impact on the environment.
- We support sustainable and safe methods of food production that reduce environmental degradation, maintain the productivity of the land over time, and support the economic viability of family farms and rural communities.
- We seek and support non-violent ways to achieve peace and justice.
- We strive to show a deep respect for human beings inside and outside our company and for the communities in which they live.[1]

3 The norms or unwritten rules guiding behaviour. For example, do employees address their boss formally or informally; are employees competitive towards each other or helpful and collaborative?

4 The language used and stories told by organizational members. For example, Wal-Mart (the US-based retail stores) now own the UK ASDA Company, both have the common yellow smiley face and 'falling prices' slogan on their US and UK TV commercials. Each have the Wal-Mart story and the ASDA story on their website.

5 Rites and ceremonies, common ways of acting and dressing. One of my students was completing an internship in a sales organization, and recounted her (uncomfortable!) experience of the monthly meeting of the sales staff. The meeting was held after work, food was provided and socializing occurred afterwards. The Sales Manager began by announcing the monthly sales goals and the actual sales of each employee. If the employee surpassed her/his goal, s/he was applauded wildly – if the employee did not meet the goal, s/he was booed. This is an example not only of a ceremony, but also the rites of *integration* (to encourage a common bond) and *enhancement* (rewarded behaviour and increased status). Other rites include the right of *passage* (orientation to the organization and its culture), and *renewal* (increasing effectiveness through training and development) (Trice and Beyer, 1984). In my first year teaching in the US, I was amazed when some of my students started turning up to class wearing colourful sashes, carrying a bat, or wearing a hat – until one of them told me it was part of *hazing* – the right of passage for becoming a sorority or fraternity member.

6 Artifacts and symbols. Think of the symbols associated with Apple Computers, Nike, UPS and McDonald's, etc., which make the organization and its products easily recognizable. Or think of possible differences in the décor of an old, traditional High Street Bank, and that of a high tech software company – how might the décor differ in expressing the values of each organization?

If you consider this list, it may strike you that as you move from the top (assumptions) to the bottom (artifacts), the aspects of culture become more observable. Edgar Schein (1985) developed a model of the three levels of organizational culture – with *assumptions* as the taken-for-granted and deepest level, *values* at the next and more accessible level, and finally *artifacts* at the most visible level. Some organizations manage their culture and image as part of their public relations. For example, did you know in the US there is a Spam Museum, a Spam Fan Club and a Spammobile that travels around the country? You may not be able to immediately identify the assumptions in your organization – these are often not expressed explicitly, but if you look around the building you work in, you can probably identify symbols – the type of décor, the letterhead on company stationary, the logo, etc. Go to the websites of organizations such as Ben and Jerry's Ice Cream, Chaparral Steel, Wal-Mart, Apple and IBM in the US, and Greenpeace, Eddie Stobart, Cadbury Chocolate, ASDA and British Nuclear Fuels in the UK. Look at the values, vision, symbols, stories and so on to see what they might tell you about the culture.

Why is Organization Culture Important?

Organizational culture is concerned with how things are done in an organization on a day-to-day basis and impacts employee relationships with their work, each other, their managers, customers and other organizational stakeholders. Culture therefore affects not only organizational performance, but also the way employees feel about their work and the organization, for example, whether they take pride in their work, or work collaboratively or competitively. Organizational culture is also tied closely to organizational identity and image – as an innovator and leader in the field, a rumbling bureaucracy-bound giant, service based on home-town values, a purveyor of the finest quality goods, or a trendy low cost retailer. Compare Richard Branson's Virgin Atlantic with British Airways, or Harrods with The Gap. So organizational culture is influential in a number of ways:

1 Organizational culture shapes the image that the public, customers, employees, shareholders and other stakeholders have of the organization. A good example of this is Eddie Stobart, a UK logistics company with a fleet of 800 trucks and 27 depots. The company differentiates itself from other haulage and warehousing companies by having its drivers wear a smart shirt and tie uniform ('professional' drivers), clean trucks noted by their green colour and each with a name, and through on time deliveries. This image is supported by the catch phrase 'Steady Eddie', and a successful fan club consisting of a 'spotters league' (truck-spotting), and where you can buy Eddie Stobart merchandise. Not your normal road haulage company!

2 Organization culture influences organizational performance. A positive culture – one that supports the image and success of the business – is important in achieving organizational goals and strategy, and meeting the demands of the environment. A negative or

counter-culture can work against organizational effectiveness. Imagine if you go to hospital for surgery and the medical and nursing staff are dressed casually in Hawaiian shirts and shorts, joking around with each other, juggling with surgical instruments, talking about experimenting on you with a new procedure, and then stop halfway through your surgery for a 'surgical chant' and commitment building activity?!

3 Organizational culture provides direction – mission, vision and core values statements identify where the organization is headed and how to get there (terminal and instrumental values). Shared values and norms help create ownership of goals, guide decision making (e.g., 'the customer is always right') and coordinate action. This can reduce the need for direct control because employees know what is expected, how to behave and what they will be rewarded for.

4 Organizational culture can help attract and retain motivated staff. Strong cultures, where organizational members agree to and buy into the culture, can have a powerful influence on behaviour and the commitment of employees. For example, Chaparral Steel, a Texas based company, have a strong culture of teamwork and autonomy. Their purpose is 'Transforming Ordinary Materials into Extraordinary Solutions', and one of their values is 'Smart Work + Hard Work + Teamwork = Excellence'.[2] However, as we will see in the later discussion about culture and ethics, strong cultures can have both positive and negative consequences.

Culture is perhaps most obvious when you start a new job in a new organization. Because you are unfamiliar with the way things are done, you notice various elements of culture that you gradually take for granted the longer you work for the company and the more socialized you become into accepted ways of doing things. These include: how to act towards other employees and your boss; particular ways of talking about work, the company and other departments; the way people dress; the stories people tell; and so on. Each organization's culture is different – Apple's culture is characterized by innovation, creativity, risk-taking and being different; IBM's culture focuses on service, professionalism, following the rules, white shirts and black suits.

Apple symbolized and played on the difference in culture with IBM in their 1984 TV Superbowl advert to introduce the then new MacIntosh computer. The advert shows a huge hazy hall full of skinheads with pale faces, dressed in grey, and watching a large screen on which a man is speaking. A young woman dressed in red and white runs down the centre of the hall and hauls a sledgehammer at the screen – which explodes... As you might guess, the young energized woman symbolizes Apple, the grey skinheads transfixed by the screen symbolize IBM.[3]

Imagine how the experience of working in these two organizations might differ?

Influences on Organizational Culture

Organizations obviously don't operate in a vacuum, but within a country and a broader society with its own values and norms. It's therefore helpful to think of culture existing at a number of levels, each of which influences the other (see Figure 3).

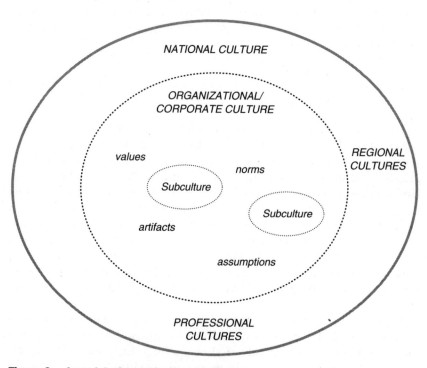

Figure 3   A model of organizational culture

National culture can therefore influence the culture of companies in terms of how organizations are design and managed. Within the national culture, we also find regional cultures, for example, the North East is different to the South East of England, and the culture in New Mexico has a strong Native American and Hispanic influence that is absent in New Hampshire. Industry and professional cultures can also have an influence on organizational culture. The culture of software professionals (GenXers) in California's Silicon Valley is different to that of mining engineers in Philadelphia. An organization's culture, while having unique qualities, is embedded within these wider values and norms and so is inevitably influenced by them because employees bring these, and their own personal values, into their work. Groups of employees (technical, professional, direct producers, managers, different departments, etc.) can have their own subcultures based on shared values and norms that may influence and are influenced by other levels and groups. So you can see that culture is quite a complex mix.

Think of the differences between the US and UK versions of the TV programme 'The Office'. Why does the US version differ? Does it relate to different cultural values and norms? What are the implications for designing and managing organizations?

National culture

The work of Geert Hofstede (1985, 2001) has been particularly influential, and will probably be discussed somewhere in your OT textbook – either in the chapter on culture or the chapter on the environment. Hofstede studied how national cultural differences influenced the IBM organizational culture in different countries. He identified four national value dimensions, later adding a fifth that led to different organizational cultures in different countries. As you read about the dimensions, think about how these might impact the way you design and manage an organization. I'll offer some suggestions to start you off:

1 *Power distance:* do members of society accept power differences and inequalities? *Small distance* focuses on equality, interdependence, accessible superiors, equal rights, participative decision making *(i.e., a flatter organization design, decentralized decision making and mutual adjustment would be more appropriate); large distance* focuses on hierarchy, privileges for those in authority, and symbols of power *(i.e., a taller organization design, centralized decision making, standardization would be more appropriate).*

2 *Uncertainty avoidance*: do members of society need certainty, caution and take action to avoid risks by providing structure and rules, etc.? *Weak avoidance* means feeling comfortable with ambiguity and lack of structure, a willingness to take risks and viewing conflict as constructive, etc. *(matrix structure, mutual adjustment ...)*; *strong avoidance* means needing formal rules and procedures, searching for consensus and job security, etc. *(functional, bureaucratic structures, formalization....)*.

3 *Individualism–collectivism*: the extent to which societies take care of their members. Is it more important to be recognized as an individual or a member of a community? *Individualism* is self-oriented and emphasizes 'I'. People value independence, initiative, clear leadership roles, tasks rather than relationships, focus on achievement, etc. *(specialization, mutual adjustment...)*; *collectivism* emphasizes social dependence, groups and communities. Institution/private life overlap, relationships are emphasized over tasks, and decisions are based on group needs.

4 *Masculinity–femininity:* the dominant values in society are masculine or feminine. Is there an emphasis on quantity, regulation and measurement...? *Masculine* values include living to work, ambition, achievement, materialism and power. Gender roles are clearly different, e.g., male assertiveness and female nurturing; *feminine* values include working to live, quality of life, consideration, social interaction, service and people.

5 *Long–short-term orientation:* do members of society pursue long-term goals and value tradition, or short-term gain and personal advantage?

These cultural differences are important for international organizations, and companies that want to internationalize, because according to Hofstede's model, the way the organization is designed and managed will vary in each country depending on the national value system. Employees of an organization in the US will be comfortable with autonomy; with being evaluated on their ability to be competitive, creative and take risks; and being expected to work long hours to finish a project (i.e., small power distance, weak uncertainty avoidance, individualism, masculinity, short-term orientation). Employees of the same organization in Brazil will be more comfortable with decisions made by those in authority; with being evaluated on their ability to follow rules; and will emphasize the importance of social interaction in getting the work done, as well as family life (i.e., large power distance, strong uncertainty avoidance, collectivism, relatively high degree of femininity).

The values of the founder

Another influence on organizational culture is the founder or CEO of the organization. For example, when we think of Virgin we think of Richard Branson. It was his vision for Virgin Records that created an organization now comprising over 200 companies in music, air travel, trains, cosmetics, space tourism, etc. Branson's values, including empowering employees and fun, underlie Virgin's culture. When we think of Microsoft we think of Bill Gates. In the 1960s he had a vision that every household and business should have a computer. In 1975, he founded Microsoft with a friend, and it has been Gates's vision that has led not only to such technological developments as the mouse and Windows, but also to Microsoft's cultural values. These include, amongst other things, innovation, product development, a work–life balance and community spirit. The latter reflect Bill Gates's philanthropic interests, and he and his wife have established the Bill and Melinda Gates Foundation which aims to reduce inequities around the world.

Some Key Issues in Studying Organizational Culture

What are some of the key areas to focus on when studying organization culture? These vary in each OT textbook, but I will summarize some of the main areas below.

What are the different types of cultures?

A number of textbooks talk about the different models and types of organizational culture. Most of these models, especially if discussed in a textbook taking a structuralist, system, and/or contingency approach (e.g., Daft, Jones) take an integrative approach – that a cohesive, values-based culture is best. The most common ones are:

Theory Z (Ouchi, 1981)   Ouchi studied Japanese management practices. **Theory Z** is based on increasing employee commitment to the organization by creating a culture of individual responsibility, collective decision making, long-term employment, a slow and long-term evaluation and promotion process, and a more humanistic approach to management through a concern for people and their work/home life.

In Search of Excellence (Peters and Waterman, 1982)   While there are many books on organizational culture, probably the most popular and well known amongst business people is this one. Peters and Waterman examined a number of 'excellent' organizations to determine what made them so, and identified eight cultural characteristics that they believed led to their success.

> A bias for action: doing rather than committeeing.
> Staying close to the customer: learn their preferences and meet them.
> Autonomy and entrepreneurship: small companies encouraged to think.
> Productivity through people: importance of best effort and rewards.
> Hands on, value driven: executives should keep in touch.
> Stick-to-the-knitting: stick with what you do best.
> Simple form, lean staff: few administrative layers.
> Loose–tight properties: dedication to core values with tolerance for play.

They see these attributes form the basis for shaping members' values and actions to create a strong and effective organization culture. Their work not only brought organizational culture to the attention of managers, but also highlighted why culture is important.

Corporate Cultures (Deal and Kennedy, 1982)   They suggested that *'strong' cultures* (where employees are committed to, and believe in, organizational goals) are important if an organization is to be successful, because they lead to high productivity and also employee satisfaction. They suggest there are five components of culture:

1   *The external environment* – the particular business environment influences the cultural style.

2   *The organization's values* – the key beliefs of the organization that should be held by all employees.

3   *The organization's heroes* – organizational members who are role models for success.

4   *The rites and rituals* – ceremonies and rituals that reinforce the organization's culture.

5 *The cultural network* – how stories, values, beliefs, etc. are communicated and shared.

Model of Four Types (Denison, 1990)

1 **Bureaucratic cultures:** focus on consistency, control, reliability, order, efficiency, conformity to rules and procedures, and maintaining the status quo (e.g. government organizations).

2 **Clan cultures:** focus on commitment, involvement, teamwork, participation, employee satisfaction and initiative (e.g. software design companies).

3 **Mission cultures:** employees oriented towards, and rewarded for, achieving the organization's clear vision, values and goals (e.g. IBM).

4 **Adaptability cultures:** focus on flexibility, innovation, risk-taking, empowerment, and learning (e.g. Apple, 3M).

You can better understand each of these different cultures by thinking about the cultural characteristics of the organization in which you work, compared to organizations you may have worked in previously. Or check out the websites of companies mentioned in this section and compare the goals, mission, vision and values statements. Also look at the symbols, language and stories you find on the website and see if these tell you anything about what type of organizational culture might exist.

Organizational culture and ethics

Organizational culture and ethical values are closely related, and most OT textbooks will include ethics within a chapter on culture. Ethical values relate to many aspects of organizational life, including: social responsibility, environmental protection, lying, rule-breaking, use of expense accounts, transparency in decision making, accuracy and misrepresentation in reporting activities, and so on. While strong organizational cultures can have a positive influence on ethical behaviour, they can equally have a negative effect.

Think about all the corporate scandals in the last 15 years – why do employees behave in unethical ways? Unethical behaviour can result from pressures to meet the demands of the economy and competitors, differing national cultural norms (e.g., whether giving and accepting gifts or bribes are appropriate), and from a strong culture that makes individual deviation from accepted norms and values very difficult. Organizational members might also get caught up in the challenge and 'rush' that they get from risking the odds. Remember Enron? The corporate culture was one of 'creative' accounting, aggressive risk-taking and invulnerability, where subsidiary companies were created with names inspired by Star Wars and Jurassic Park characters, such as Raptor and Chewco. So there are aspects of culture, particularly strong cultures, that are conducive to unethical behaviour, and ethical breaches occur when individuals feel unable or unwilling to question those 'normal' practices.

Many organizations have an ethics code of conduct, and are explicit about their ethical values. Chaparral Steel, the Texas-based company mentioned earlier, has amongst its values:

1 Create a climate in which ethics are so integral to day-to-day operations that ethical behaviour is self-enforcing. Management will lead by example by designing organizations, policies and procedures that make it easier rather than harder to do the right thing. The company will have a reputation among its customers, competitors and investors as a fair, honest and reliable firm with which to do business.

2 Be a responsible member of the community. The company and its employees will take pride in their communities and be actively involved in community affairs. Company facilities will maintain a neat and aesthetically pleasing appearance.

3 Be environmentally responsible; proactively supporting, protecting and improving the environment and encouraging the recycling of natural resources.[4]

But it is not enough for an organization to formalize their ethical values and what constitutes ethical behaviour, the values need to be communicated, monitored and enacted. Ethical dilemmas arise when values are in conflict, where norms work against ethical behaviour, or systems are not aligned with ethical action. It is therefore important to *ensure that the organization's structure, culture and systems support ethical action.* For example, the organization might have values that include customer service and teamwork, but if employees are given individual bonuses for getting sales or making deals regardless of cost, then the reward system will work against the values.

Can culture be managed?

This is a key question and one that you may be asked in an exam or as an essay assignment. If you think about what we've already discussed, the answer is – well, sort of! I'm not being facetious here – think of the section on the impact of national culture on organizational culture... the answer here is that an organization opening a division in a different country will have to think about how the organization can be designed and managed because the country will have it's own cultural values. Remember the controversy over EuroDisney in Paris, which was criticized for trying to impose US cultural values on French culture? Disney made changes in the requirements of employees at EuroDisney to better adapt to cultural differences in France. Also, a Project Manager in a multinational organization, who was responsible for a design team consisting of members in the US and Europe told me of his initial shock during a teleconference with team members when the European team members left at 5pm – until he realized this was a cultural norm. So organizational culture is not entirely manageable.

On the other hand, managers can shape culture through vision and values statements, etc., through their actions and expectations, by creating systems that support the organization's values, and by structuring the organization in particular ways, for example, organic or mechanistic. We've mentioned that some cultures can be more productive than others, so the assumption underlying the management of culture is that leaders can create or transform cultures that are effective. Peters and Waterman's premise was that organizations can adopt the characteristics of 'excellent companies' through mimetic isomorphism or the modeling of behaviours and practices. This relates to institutional theory, which we will talk about in the section on strategy. So if we think back to contingency approaches, the underlying assumption of many studies of organization culture is that *if we understand what culture is, how it's shaped, and the various models or types of culture, we can then create an organizational culture that is most effective in the circumstances* (given the environment and business strategy). Managers may also need to transform their organization culture as environmental demands change (economic, market, legal, technical, etc.), a new CEO is hired with different values to the old CEO, or they find ineffective and/or unethical practices.

A related question is whether culture can be over-managed? In other words can it become so trite that employees find it laughable? If you've ever watched the film *Office Space*, you might get a sense of this when Jennifer Aniston's character (a restaurant waitperson) is told by her manager that she doesn't have enough 'flair' – buttons (badges) on her uniform. Flair is supposed to allow employees to express themselves and create a fun atmosphere. Aniston's character only has 15 pieces of flair (the minimum required), whereas another waitperson has 37 and a terrific smile – a fact the manager is at pains to point out! In other words, culture can be overmanaged to the point that employees resist conforming.

Contemporary Approaches to Organizational Culture

Up to now, we have looked at structuralist and contingency theories that take an integrative approach to culture – a cohesive, values-based culture (e.g., Ouchi, Peters and Waterman). Remember also that these studies assume that culture can be managed to the benefit of the organization. More contemporary approaches including interpretive (social constructionist) and postmodern approaches, view culture as pluralistic and fragmented. Essentially, the integrative approach might talk about subcultures having their own values and norms, but that these generally support the organizational culture. The focus is on having a strong culture into which organizational members are socialized, and to which they are committed. Interpretive studies of culture suggest that there are multiple meanings across groups and individuals, and explore different interpretations and meanings. Interpretive researchers often do ethnographies of organizational life, talking to people, collecting stories, attending meetings, and so on. Tony Watson (2001: 114–18), whose work I mentioned in Part 1, talks about two competing cultural discourses (ways of talking and looking at the world) in the organization he studied – the official (empowerment and growth) and the unofficial (control costs and jobs). Managers switched between the two. The implications are that in reality, culture is not a cohesive set of meanings and values, and indeed, as you will see, postmodern conceptualizations assume a far more fragmented and conflictual perspective of culture.

Let's look at three contemporary approaches to the study of organizational culture that have offered an alternative perspective and raised some interesting issues: symbolic, narrative and postmodern. Symbolic studies of culture focus on Schein's (1985) most visible level of artifacts and symbols, and the meanings they carry. They also look at culture as performance. Narrative approaches can (but not always) be seen as part of Burrell and Morgan's (1979) interpretive paradigm. They are often based on the notion that people shape culture (shared and taken-for-granted ways of understanding, seeing and doing things) in their everyday interactions. Culture cannot be generalized across organizations, but is contextualised to a particular organization because shared and multiple meanings emerge in relation to the particular group of people and to the mission and vision statements, symbols, images, actions, interactions, values, stories, language, etc. We can therefore explore an organization's culture by studying how organizational members make meaning in and from interactions, symbols, artifacts, stories and narratives.

Culture as symbolism and performance

A number of studies of culture are grounded in *dramaturgy* – an idea developed by Erving Goffman, a Canadian sociologist. He suggested we accomplish meaning through social interaction, and that social interaction is a performance. He used the theatrical metaphor as a means of studying how individuals shape social realities, suggesting that we are all actors engaged in a performance of reality, as if on stage. From a dramaturgical perspective, organizations are studied using drama as a metaphor, a means of shedding light on culture, or organizations are seen as social dramas or 'theatres' consisting of many different performances coordinated to achieve organizational goals. Those in authority manage these performances as they define the roles and scripts of others. Goffman himself studied how individuals in institutions, for example hospitals, conform and adapt to formal organizational performances.

Another example of culture as symbolism and performance is the well-known American study of an advertising agency by Michael Rosen. He uses the idea of *social drama* to analyse how organizational culture is communicated through symbols, dress, language and pictures, and how the rituals associated with an annual business breakfast maintain the culture and reinforce asymmetrical power relationships. As you might imagine, there are some colourful and intriguing studies of culture from this perspective!

Narrative and storytelling

The simplest way of defining *narrative* is as a story of real events, with a plot and characters which, when analysed, will tell us about the organization, its culture and practices. Narrative-based work often identifies the narratives and stories told by organizational members, explores how they construct and reproduce meaning, and how they help organizational members make sense of their organizational lives. You might come across the work of David Boje, Ellen O'Connor, Yiannis Gabriel and Tony Watson, who look at the various types of stories, plots, characters, heroes and villains, and how they shape meaning and culture.

Postmodern perspectives on culture

You may remember from Part 1 that postmodern approaches to organization theory question the idea that there is an external, commonly shared social reality, suggesting instead that social life is value-less and image-driven. If your textbook takes a critical or postmodern approach to culture, then you will probably be exposed to the following ideas about culture:

- Intertexuality – culture is text (which is everything: discourse, documents, events, actions, etc.) constructed by multiple discourses, authors and readings. Therefore meanings and values are always shifting and there is no unified organization culture.
- Fragmentation – culture is fragmented, shifting and a hollow performance in which nothing is real and everything is contested. There are no shared values. Culture is simulacra, images and performances in which there are no originals.
- Polyphony – culture consists of many voices all speaking at once.
- Ideological – culture carries meanings that privilege elite groups (managers, shareholders) and marginalize others. Organization culture is an attempt to control employees. Ideologies need to be surfaced and deconstructed to reveal assumptions, contradictions, unstable meanings, etc.

David Boje (2001), an American postmodern organizational theorist, suggests that organizational researchers need to study both narratives and antenarratives in organizations. He defines antenarratives as pre-stories that refuse to be coherent and are fragmented, temporary and partial understandings. He compares antenarratives to the play *Tamara*, in which audience members follow different characters telling different stories across different stages. Each member of the audience leaves the play with a different story, and a different interpretation. He suggests that organizations are like *Tamara*, because organizational members similarly chase, tell and negotiate stories over times, places and people. Whereas stories have plots, antenarratives contain no agreement on plot and struggles emerge over whose plot takes precedence. There is therefore no collective organizational culture, only *fragmentation*. Boje suggests we can still study culture if we look at different narrations of stories. As an example, he analyses the various themes identified in narratives told by members of a Southwestern Science Laboratory where he found 'official' narratives, informal counternarratives, and competing claims for coherence as storytellers tried to manage and supplant narratives.

INTEGRATIVE CASE

Let's go to our restaurant and think about the cultural characteristics that might be most effective. Recall that you have a flat organization, integration is through direct contact (you have only 30 employees), you make most of the decisions, there's little formalization, and given this, and the fact you are in the entrepreneurial or start up stage of your restaurant's life cycle, you have a fairly organic structure. So if you want to shape a culture that supports your goals, blends with your current structure, and generates employee commitment, what might you consider? You might be particularly interested in Peters and Waterman's ideas about staying close to your customers and sticking to the knitting because you are dependent on the tastes and preferences of your local clientele. Would a clan culture be more appropriate? Why?

You might find it useful to work through the material in this chapter and think about how you would consider the issues in relation to your restaurant. Think about the following questions:

1 What will be your terminal values (e.g., profitability, social responsibility) and instrumental values (e.g., teamwork, courtesy, more than meeting customer expectations)?

2 How will you communicate these, through a written vision, mission and values statement given at orientation (rite of passage), hung on the wall (symbol) and through your own behaviour?

3 Will you have on the spot rewards for employees who enact these values e.g., tickets to the theatre for an employee who more than meets a customer's expectations?

4 Will you have a logo, a dress code, a 'Thank-you' or holiday party, and so on?

(Continued)

> *(Continued)*
>
> **5** Might you have particular symbols or artifacts as part of your culture?
>
> These are all ways in which culture emerges and meanings are created.
>   Also think about how you might look at the culture of the restaurant from the different perspectives: structuralist, symbolism and performance, and postmodern. How might these perspectives offer different insights?

USING THE MATERIAL

Your textbook will go into more detail than the overview in this chapter. As you read the material, consider it from two perspectives:

- Why is culture important and what are the implications for designing and managing organizations and for organizational effectiveness?
- How culture relates to the environment, strategy, structure and technology.

You will also find it helpful to think of examples to bring the concepts to life. Think of your own organization and work experience. Look around at the symbols, décor, artifacts, etc. See if you have a mission, vision and values statement and what they tell you about the culture. Listen to the way people talk and the language they use. Are the formal values enacted – if so, how and if not, why not? One of the assignments I give in class asks students to do this, and they often comment that they see things they've never noticed before. Another way of grounding the concepts is to think about any organizational culture change you might have experienced, how the change was implemented and whether it was effective. You might have experienced a new CEO, Division Manager, Dean, or other senior manager who has attempted to influence and change organizational culture or sub-cultures. Grounding the concepts should help you understand them.
    Questions you might be asked include:

1 Can culture be managed? What are the possible advantages and disadvantages of managing culture?

This is addressed in the relevant section above – and you should also discuss the impact (positive and negative) of culture on ethical practices in organizations. If your textbook takes a multiple or critical perspective, then you should consider the postmodern notion of culture as a form of control, and the idea that if culture is simulacra, polyphonic and intertextual, then it becomes impossible to manage because it is always shifting.

2 Discuss why organizational culture and ethics are interrelated. How can managers create an ethical culture?

Review the ideas in the section on 'Organizational culture and ethics'.

3 What might you do to build a strong organizational culture?

Begin by stating what a strong culture is and why you might want one. Then discuss how you can create a strong culture through goals, mission, vision, values statements, language, rites and ceremonies, artifacts, etc. Give examples either from your own experience, your textbook, or the Internet. Look at some of the issues in the section on 'Can culture be managed?'.

Taking it **FURTHER**

Contemporary approaches to organizational culture obviously raise some very different issues:

1 How might you study organization culture as performance? Who are the actors, and what are some of the performances in your organization?
2 Can you identify narratives, antenarratives and counternarratives in your organization?
3 Is organizational culture just another way of controlling employees without them being aware they are being controlled?

Notes

1 http://www.benjerry.com, accessed 2 December, 2006.
2 http://www.chaparralsteel.com/CompanyOverview/CorporatePhilosophy. html, Chaparral Steel vision, values, etc., accessed 16 November, 2006.
3 You can see this at http://www.uiowa.edu/~commstud/adclass/1984_ mac_ad.html, accessed 16 November, 2006.

4   http://www.chaparralsteel.com/CompanyOverview/CorporatePhilosophy.
html, accessed 16 November, 2006.

Textbook Guide

DAFT: *Chapter 10.*
HATCH WITH CUNLIFFE: *Chapter 6.*
JONES: *Chapters 2 and 7.*
WATSON: *Chapters 3, 4 and 7.*

Additional Reading

Boje, D. M. (1995) 'Stories of the storytelling organization: a postmodern analysis of Disney as Tamara-land', *Academy of Management Journal,* 38: 997–1035.

Boje, D. M. (2001) *Narrative Methods for Organizational and Communication Research.* London: Sage.

Czarniawska, B. (1997) *Narrating the Organization: Dramas of Institutional Identity.* Chicago: University of Chicago Press.

Deetz, S. A., Tracy, S. J. and Simpson, J. L. (2000) *Leading Organizations Through Transition: Communication and Cultural Change.* Thousand Oaks, CA: Sage (takes a social constructionist approach and addresses the role of language).

Goffman, E. (1959) *The Presentation of Self in Everyday Life.* Garden City, NY: Doubleday.

Linstead, S. A. and Grafton-Small, R. (1992) 'On reading organizational culture', *Organization Studies,* 13: 331–56.

Martin, J. (2002) *Organizational Culture: Mapping the Terrain.* Thousand Oaks, CA: Sage.

Martin, J. and Frost, P. (1996) 'The organization culture war games: a struggle for intellectual dominance', in S. R. Clegg and C. Hardy (eds), *Studying Organization: Theory and Method.* London: Sage. pp. 345–67.

O'Connor, E. S. (2000) 'Plotting the organization: the embedded narrative as a construct for studying change', *Journal of Applied Behavioral Science,* 36: 174–93.

Rosen, M. (1985) 'Breakfast at Spiros: dramaturgy and dominance', *Journal of Management,* 11: 31–48.

4	
environment and strategy	

Many OT textbooks cover environment and strategy in separate chapters, and somewhere near the beginning of the book. I've found that for many students, strategy and the environment tend to be pretty nebulous because they seem far removed from everyday experience. So I cover structure, technology and culture first, because most students have worked in, or been a customer of, an organization so have experience in which they can ground the concepts. You can also observe culture. Then I move on to environment and strategy – which I've always found easier to understand if I think of them together – because strategy is a way of responding to, and managing, the environment. **Organizational environment** is usually defined as the general forces or elements existing outside the organization, but which might have an influence on its survival and operation. **Strategy** is the plan, decisions and actions identified as being necessary to achieving organizational goals. You will also come across a number of additional terms (e.g. **boundary spanning, buffering**) – be sure to check out the definitions in the Glossary. These will help you navigate the course material. As usual, I'll highlight the key concepts and theories in each, and then address the relationship between environment, strategy and structure.

The Environment: Key Concepts

Most OT textbooks discuss the various elements of the organizational environment in some depth and as these are straightforward I will not redescribe them here. Instead, let's focus on the relationship between the organization and it's environment, and why this is important. Figure 4 offers a way to make sense of all the various elements, and how they relate to each other.

The organization carries out its activities in a *domain*, which is part of the wider physical, political, economic, etc. environment. The domain is the part of the environment that the organization interacts with on

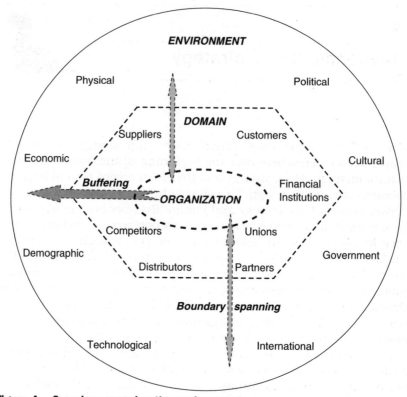

Figure 4   Overview: mapping the environment

a regular basis and has some influence over, for example, products, suppliers, customers, etc. In order to survive, senior managers and decision makers in organizations have to monitor the environment *(boundary spanning)* and take action to protect the organization from environmental uncertainties *(buffering)*. The environment surrounding the organization can influence the organization's survival by creating uncertainty and requiring the organization to adapt to changing demands and increasing complexity. An organization attempts to achieve its goals and deal with environmental demands through its organization or business *strategy*. However, not all senior managers and decision makers will perceive their surrounding environment and the degree of uncertainty in the same way. This can be related to the amount of information managers have about the environment – when they have little information then the environment is seen to be uncertain and unpredictable.

Let's look at some of the influences. Uncertainty can be created in a number of ways:

1 **Environmental complexity.** Environmental complexity relates to the number and the range of elements affecting an organization. The greater the number and range, the more complex the environment. A multinational organization with a wide range of products and services has to deal with multiple markets, economies and suppliers; varying government regulations; and differing social, demographic and cultural factors. This requires many boundary spanning activities in each country and across the organization as a whole, as well as a need to focus on buffering activities to ensure that production continues regardless of demands.

2 **Environmental stability.** Stability relates to the rate of environmental change the organization faces. Some organizations operate within stable environments because there is little competition, few technological developments, and the customer base is unchanging. Public sector government organizations often operate in relatively stable conditions. The Department of Motor Vehicles is a good example: the service doesn't change, there is no competition, technological developments might require a change in work process but this is likely to be relatively rare and occur over a long period of time.

3 **Environmental richness.** Richness refers to the amount and availability of resources. Such resources might include raw materials, experienced and qualified labour, and financial resources.

So we can compare environmental complexity, stability and richness for organizations such as a chocolate manufacturer, where the environment is relatively simple and stable (chocolate rarely changes in terms of raw materials), to an airline company having to address a competitive environment, increasing fuel costs, changing demands on its operation and declining markets because of terrorism. An analysis of the environment is therefore important because *the more complex and unstable the environment, the more the organization will need a structure, strategy and internal processes to adapt to and manage change.* This will include designing a structure, planning a business strategy, creating an organizational culture, and establishing processes and systems to facilitate environmental scanning, information collection, flexibility, responsiveness and innovation.

Let's have a look at some general guidelines you should be able to pull out of your textbook:

1 The more complex and unstable the environment the more likely the organization will need boundary spanning and buffering activities. These might include establishing industry associations, lobbying government, and so on.

2 Organizations try to gain control over necessary resources to better manage environmental uncertainty – this is known as *Resource Dependence Theory*.

3 Organizations are better able to survive if they focus on meeting **stakeholder** requirements and needs – this is known as *Institutional Theory*.

4 Organizations try to minimize the costs of transactions with the environment and within the organization – this is known as *Transaction Cost Theory*.

5 Organizations compete for survival and have to adapt to survive – this is known as *Population Ecology*.

6 As a means of managing environmental complexity and instability, organizations can form strategic alliances, joint ventures and network organizations (see Part 2, section 1).

Resource dependence theory

Resource dependence theory (Pfeffer and Salancik, 1978) is based on the idea that organizations need to control the resources they need in order to survive. The greater the control an organization has over those resources, the less dependent it will be on organizations who do. If you are a beer brewing company dependent on suppliers to provide you with raw materials including hops and barley, you will want to increase your influence over those resources, or you could be at the mercy of your suppliers. You might also want to increase control over the outlets for your beer, e.g., pubs, restaurants and liquor stores. There are many ways of doing this, including:

• Establishing a partnership, acquire or merge with a supplier or competitor. You may remember from the previous chapter that US-based Wal-Mart bought

UK-based ASDA, which allowed them to expand into international markets and expanded the products base in the US by bringing in ASDA products.
- Finding multiple suppliers as a means of minimizing dependence on one.
- Creating a joint venture with suppliers (vertical integration).
- Creating a joint venture or strategic alliance with competitors (horizontal integration).
- Changing the organization's environmental domain, for example finding new markets, manufacturing a different product not subject to government regulation.

So resource dependence theory states that an organization has to minimize its dependence on other organizations and maximize its control over the resources of other organizations.

Institutional theory

Institutional theory addresses how organizations adapt to the political and social values and demands of their institutional environment. Institutional theorists suggest organizations thrive if they can satisfy the demands, and thereby establish their legitimacy (i.e., accepted as doing the right thing) in the eyes of their stakeholders (customers, shareholders, investors, government, etc.). So organizations in the same institutional environment might develop similar structures, practices and processes to deal with the demands. This similarity between organizations is known as *isomorphism*, and is seen to occur in three main ways:

1. *Coercive isomorphism.* Organizations adopt similar practices because of laws, regulations, political sanctions or public outcry. For example, in response to the recent corporate scandals and decreasing public trust, the US Government passed the Sarbanes-Oxley Act in 2002, which amongst other things requires CEOs, and CFOs to certify the truth of annual and quarterly financial reports. Also, public outcry about child labour practices in third world countries have forced organizations to reconsider their suppliers and outsourcing, or to establish labour requirement standards for suppliers.

2. *Mimetic isomorphism.* Organizations imitate (mimic) the practices of other successful organizations to ensure their survival. This can be particularly useful for new organizations that have no experience dealing with environmental demands. Remember the boom and bust of Silicon Valley – an example of a situation where mimetic isomorphism didn't occur? Many Silicon Valley companies failed because they had no well-established high tech (apart from Apple)

and dot com companies with a long and successful institutional history that they could imitate. New start up companies consisted of young, creative entrepreneurs with great ideas, but little knowledge about how to manage stakeholder demands and concerns. Many companies foundered and tried to hire in experienced managers – often too late.

3 *Normative isomorphism.* Organizations adopt the norms and values of other successful companies in their domain. This might be through professional or industry associations, hiring in managers from other companies, benchmarking or publications.

In the US, Wal-Mart is a good example of an organization that has been finding itself having to adapt to their institutional environment. Their legitimacy – based on a 'Home Town America' image – has been affected by bad press relating to claims of importing products and to a number of sexual harassment and discrimination lawsuits. Residents in States such as California, have successfully organized opposition to new Wal-Mart stores in their locality. So Wal-Mart has had to focus on increasing its legitimacy in the eyes of its stakeholders.

Transaction cost theory

Transaction cost theory looks at the cost and the strategies used to manage the relationship between the organization and its environment. It's based on the idea that companies try to control and minimize the costs associated with the exchange of resources between an organization and its environment, and the costs of production or providing a service. The latter takes us back to section 1 and the organizational design issues of integration and differentiation. Let's take our integrative case as an example. As the owner of the restaurant, you will need to negotiate with your suppliers, who will include suppliers of vegetables, meat, fish, alcohol and equipment, plus phone, energy, advertising, etc. companies. You will continually monitor the exchange to try to make sure you are getting a good deal and being supplied with a quality and cost effective product. If you discover your meat supplier is sending inferior cuts of meat, or the phone company suddenly reduces the level of service and increases costs, then you will need to renegotiate contracts. The time and money spent doing this are *external transaction costs*. There are also *internal transaction costs* because you have to liaise with the Assistant

Manager, Chef, cooks and bar staff to determine and coordinate what supplies are needed, by when. Imagine the complexity of managing external and internal transactions in large organizations. One of the ways of doing so are through strategic alliances and joint ventures (see section 1) where organizations collaborate to share the costs associated with product development and/or competing with other organizations.

Population ecology

In OT, population ecologists study how organizations producing similar products or services (a *population*) adapt – or do not adapt – to their environment. Based on Darwin's theory of evolution and the survival of the fittest, the population ecology model states that new organizations try to find a *niche*, a unique need and pool of resources in the environment. New organizations survive if they adapt to the continual changes in their population, and these changes occur in stages:

1 *Variation*. New organizations appear in a population.

2 *Selection*. Some of the new organizations survive because they are 'selected' or suited to the environment. These organizations might take business away from more established organizations. For example, low cost, no-frills airlines (EasyJet, Jet2, JetBlue, Ryanair, Southwest, etc.) have had an impact on the way many traditional airlines now do business (e.g., pricing, online ticketing, no in-flight meals) and on traffic at smaller airports. Those organizations that do not fit environmental needs fail or enter a new niche.

3 *Retention*. Organizations are retained (valued) by the environment.

Population ecology differs from resource dependence theory because it focuses on the environment rather than the organization, that is, on whether the environmental characteristics 'select' or support the organization. Resource dependence theory focuses on how the organization manages its environment.

Essentially, these theories suggest that *an organization's success depends on its ability to manage – or adapt to – its environment*. This issue is addressed in the next model we will look at, which focuses on the birth, growth and death of organizations.

Organizational growth (Greiner, 1972)

Organization theorists have suggested that just as we humans grow and develop, so too do organizations, and they have identified a number of stages that organizations pass through as they grow in size. This is known as the *organizational life cycle* model, which suggests that there is a correlation between the age of an organization and its size. It was initially developed as having five stages in the 1970s by Greiner and has been added to by researchers over the years. You might find this model described in the chapter on environment, strategy, structure or change, because it relates to each. We will discuss the topic here, because growth and development will relate to environmental opportunities and demands, and how well the organization adapts to them. It will also take us into the relationship between environment and organizational design factors. Please review the main elements in the Life Cycle Model explained in your textbook, which will cover a description of each stage of growth and the associated problems. What we will do here is look at their implications for structure and design. We will begin at the early stages of an organization's evolution:

1 The creativity or entrepreneurial stage: This is the start-up of the organization, where survival in terms of establishing a market niche and customer base is key. At this stage, high uncertainty is likely, especially in a competitive environment, as the owner(s) of the company tries to identify and make use of environmental opportunities by seeking funding, trying to establish a market niche and a company direction. If the company grows, there is often a *'Leadership' crisis* because the owners have to shift their focus from the product or service to the management of the company – and this requires a different focus and set of skills. At this stage, the company will be small, probably with the following characteristics:

- A flat organization – few levels in the hierarchy (low vertical differentiation) and a fairly wide span of control (high horizontal differentiation) because the owner(s) will be focusing personally on bringing their ideas to fruition and getting the business up and running. People will be added as skills are needed.
- Integration – direct contact as the owner keeps personal contact and day-to-day involvement with every aspect of the business.
- Centralization – Centralized decision making by the owner.
- Mutual adjustment – in the early stages of company growth, new, unique issues and problems will arise that need to be dealt with as they occur.
- Low formalization – little need for written rules, policies and job descriptions because employees are figuring out what needs to be done and how.
- Organic – as the owner and employees attempt to establish the company.

2 The direction or collectivity stage: At this stage survival may depend on how well the organization is coping with environmental as well as internal demands: can the company generate revenue, maintain and grow a market share, develop buffering and boundary activities? Common goals, departments, teams and roles develop. Employees are committed to the organization. An *'Autonomy' crisis* arises as employees want more responsibility and the owner and top management may be reluctant to relinquish any control.

- Taller organization – more managers are hired (vertical differentiation) and departments are created (horizontal differentiation), as the owner needs more help and expertise in managing an expanding business. A functional structure often emerges.
- Integration – some direct contact but some clarification of reporting relationships and responsibilities as an increase in size makes coordination and communication more difficult.
- De/centralization – decisions still made by the owner and perhaps top managers.
- Mutual adjustment – as new problems are still being encountered, new employees, new customers, etc.
- Low formalization – still, but some formal communication processes and systems are developed to cope with increasing number of employees.
- Organic – because the owner and top managers are still establishing the company, dealing with new situations, and need to be flexible in meeting changing demands.

3 The delegation or collectivity stage: In response to the autonomy crisis, authority is delegated down the organization. In order to maintain some control yet allow for cost reduction and innovation, individual performance and rewards are linked to organizational performance (e.g. stock options). A *crisis of 'Control'* may occur as top managers and functional managers vie for power and control over resources. The organization will also need to maintain buffering and boundary management activities to ensure stakeholder needs are being met.

- Flatter organization – more departments may be created, or the organization might move to a divisional or multi-divisional structure to balance delegation, product improvement and financial responsibility. Specialists such as Human Resource Managers, Product Designers are needed to deal with increasing requirements and the need to maintain market growth (horizontal differentiation).
- Integration – clarification of reporting relationships, rules, procedures.
- Decentralization – decisions delegated to divisional and technical managers.
- Mutual adjustment – within newly created divisions as they respond to shifting markets, new products, new goals, growth, etc. But some standardization at a corporate level to maintain control.

- Higher formalization – as top managers establish reporting mechanisms, and performance management systems to ensure divisions focus on overall company strategy.
- Organic/mechanistic – as the organization tries to balance delegation with control. A management power struggle might result in a move towards a mechanistic structure as top management try to regain control.

4 The coordination or formalization stage: As the organization grows, so does the need to balance control and delegation, and for more formal systems, procedures, rules and specialist knowledge. A balance is needed between divisional and corporate goals. As this continues, a *'Red Tape' crisis* can arise because if too many rules and systems are established, then creativity and flexibility are stifled. This can inhibit an organization's responsiveness to environmental demands, especially if the environment is complex and unstable.

- Taller organization – the number of levels in the hierarchy may increase as senior managers focus on strategy and planning, and middle and lower managers on operations (vertical differentiation).
- Integration – task forces and liaison roles are required to coordinate the effort of departments and work on problems. Corporate management might establish policies, procedures and direct contact between divisional heads to encourage collaboration between divisions.
- Decentralization – responsibilities may be pushed further down the organization to those who have the expertise to deal with complex problems. But control mechanisms are in place to monitor decisions and ensure they benefit the company as a whole.
- Standardization – within divisions, but also from a corporate level to maintain a corporate perspective.
- Formalization – formal written policies, plans, rules, procedures and systems are required to ensure consistency within divisions and across the organization, timely decision making, and clear goals and roles, etc.
- Mechanistic – the organization becomes more mechanistic as differentiation and formalization increase.

5 The collaboration or elaboration stage: The organization deals with the red tape crisis by reorganizing into smaller, more manageable and more personal units. At this stage a *'crisis of renewal'* may occur as employees suffer stress resulting from change, uncertainty and ambiguity.

- Flatter organization – emerges as a smaller product-based divisional or a matrix structure is used to support increased customer responsiveness.
- Integration – face-to-face, direct contact. Teamwork.
- Decentralization – decisions made at the point of contact to encourage responsiveness and innovation, and streamline decision making.

- Mutual adjustment – so each unit can respond to customer needs.
- Less formalization – greater focus on trust, teamwork and autonomy.
- Organic – all of the above results in a more organic structure.

Greiner suggests that the result may be a renewed and viable organization (for example, a new divisional or matrix structure) or the organization's demise. Also, as you might have guessed, there is a link to our next section because an organization's strategy will change depending on its stage of growth.

Organizational Strategy: Key Concepts

Strategy is a whole separate discipline within the field of organization studies, and so many OT textbooks will highlight the essentials of business strategy and focus on the relationship between strategy and design. That's what we will summarize here. An organization's *business strategy* should set the direction of the organization, identify how the organization will manage environmental demands, and determine the internal organizational processes and practices necessary to achieve the goals. An effective strategy will also utilize and develop the organization's core competencies (skills, expertise, resources) in order to meet it's goals. Determining strategy involves analysing the relationship between the organization and it's environment: an environmental assessment of the demands, opportunities and threats, and an internal assessment of the organization's goals, strengths and weaknesses – a *SWOT* analysis (strengths, weaknesses, opportunities and threats). The organization will develop a strategy depending on the results.

OT textbooks cover different types of strategies:

Competitive strategies (Porter, 1980)

Michael Porter identified three competitive strategies, arguing that companies needed to adopt the strategy that gives them the best strategic advantage:

1 *Low-cost leadership*: competing through lower costs, e.g. EasyJet aims to be a leader in low-cost scheduled air services across Europe, and have teamed up with other companies to provide low-cost car rental and holiday accommodation. The US's Southwest Airline competes by offering low fares, on-time arrivals and safe flights. They keep costs low by not flying into major airports, using a

shuttle approach (i.e. planes land at airports to drop off and pick up passengers. Some passengers stay on the plane at these airports to get to their final destination) and offer a no-frills meal service.

2 *Differentiation*: offering a unique service or product to differentiate from other organizations, e.g., Jaguar differentiate their cars from others by their long ancestry, high-class comfort, powerful and sleek image, and emphasis on craftsmanship quality.

3 *Focus*: focus on a selected customer group or geographic region. This can be a focused low-cost strategy or a focused differentiation strategy. In the US, Chuck E Cheese's is a national restaurant that focuses on kids and families. You can book a birthday party, which includes pizza, games, activities and costumed characters!

As I mentioned in the introduction to the environment section the way managers perceive the environment and the degree of uncertainty will influence strategy. Not only will managers want to try to influence and control the resources in their environmental domain (resource dependence), they will try to minimize the costs associated with managing the exchanges (transaction cost). So in terms of strategy, this means thinking about the costs and benefits of the following:

- Finding a niche and starting a new organization.
- Protecting and/or enlarging the organization's domain through a focus strategy on a specific domain or diversifying and entering a new domain.
- Establishing strategic alliances and joint ventures as a means of increasing competitiveness and/or developing new products.
- Expanding markets domestically or internationally while balancing the increased external and internal transaction costs.
- Adapting to changes in the population.

The Link Between Environment, Strategy, Structure and Culture

Figure 5 illustrates the link between environment, strategy, organization structure, design and culture. This takes us back to the statement in Part 1 that every topic in OT is related to the other: organizational effectiveness will depend on whether the organization develops a structure, design and culture that allows it to respond to and manage its environment.

We have already talked about the need for business strategy to be based on an external analysis of the environment and an internal analysis of organizational competencies. The unique set of external and internal

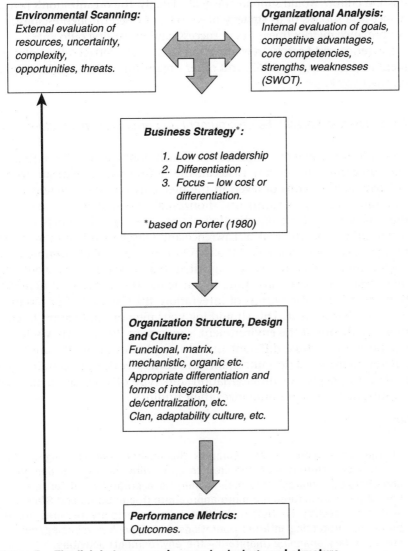

Environmental Scanning:
External evaluation of
resources, uncertainty,
complexity,
opportunities, threats.

Organizational Analysis:
Internal evaluation of goals,
competitive advantages,
core competencies,
strengths, weaknesses
(SWOT).

Business Strategy*:

1. Low cost leadership
2. Differentiation
3. Focus – low cost or
   differentiation.

*based on Porter (1980)

**Organization Structure, Design
and Culture:**
Functional, matrix,
mechanistic, organic etc.
Appropriate differentiation and
forms of integration,
de/centralization, etc.
Clan, adaptability culture, etc.

Performance Metrics:
Outcomes.

Figure 5   The link between environment, strategy and structure

characteristics facing the organization will determine whether the business
strategy should be low-cost leadership, differentiation, or focus. This in turn
will influence which organization structure will be most effective. For example, low-cost leadership is often associated with a functional structure
and its associated design factors. In this type of structure, a bureaucratic or

mission culture would support the goals. Finally, the organization's performance and success of its strategy need to be assessed through establishing performance metrics (measures of success) and measuring outcomes.

Lawrence and Lorsch drew attention to the link between the environment and structure in 1967, and other organization theorists have built on their work.

Lawrence and Lorsch: the environment and organization structure

I mentioned Lawrence and Lorsch when looking at differentiation and integration in section 1. Recall the notion that organizations are differentiated in terms of levels in the hierarchy (vertical differentiation) and functions or departments (horizontal differentiation), and that this will vary in each organization – some are tall and others are flat organizations. We will look at Lawrence and Lorsch's work in more depth here because they focused on the effect of the external environment on organization structure. They suggested that organizations would be more effective if their structure, in particular the degree of differentiation and the resulting forms of integration, fits the level of uncertainty of their environment. This should jog your memory in relation to contingency theory (*if* the environment is uncertain, *then...*)! They selected ten firms from three different industries, plastics (a highly uncertain environment), food (less uncertain) and container (least uncertain), and studied the degree of differentiation and type of integration in each organization. Table 6 summarizes their findings.

So:

1 The more uncertain and complex the environment, the higher the level of differentiation required to cope with the various demands and changes required. This means there is a greater need for integration. Organic structures are more appropriate (recall Burns and Stalker's work from section 1). Note also that high uncertainty requires more *buffering* (protecting internal operations from shock purchasing/sales) and *boundary spanning* (monitoring the environment) activities.

2 In stable and less complex environments, a lower level of differentiation and integration and a more standardized organization structure are required. Mechanistic structures are therefore more appropriate.

However, Lawrence and Lorsch didn't just look at organization structure, they focused on three departments in each company – production, R & D and sales, and found that at the department level, differentiation occurred

Table 6   The relationship between environmental uncertainty, differentiation and integration

Industry	Environment	Differentiation	Integration
Plastics	High uncertainty – rapid technological and product change.	Requires a *high degree of differentiation* to meet demands.	High need for integration – low formalization, decentralized decision making and direct communication to deal with problems, mutual adjustment.
Food	Moderate uncertainty – stable technology, some new products.	Moderate differentiation.	Moderate to low integration.
Container	Low uncertainty – standard products, little change.	Requires *low differentiation* as fewer environmental demands.	Low integration – integration through formal rules and procedures, centralized decision making, standardized procedures and practices.

Based on Lawrence and Lorsch (1967) Reprinted by permission of *Harvard Business Review*. From "Organization and Environment: Managing Differentiation and Integration" by P.R. Lawrence and J.W. Lorsch, 1967. Copyright © 1967 by the Harvard Business School Publishing Corporation; all rights reserved.

in relation to goals, time orientation, formality of structure, interpersonal orientation, attitudes and ways of operating. Departments operating in relatively stable environments (e.g. production) were more formal and structured than those in less stable environments (e.g. sales). R & D had a longer time orientation as they were working on lengthy projects, while production had a shorter time orientation based on daily, weekly or monthly targets. These differences can cause conflict between departments unless integration occurs (e.g. schedules, cross-department task forces).

Some general guidelines

Let's draw out some general guidelines about the relationship between environment, strategy, structure, design and culture. These will be addressed in various chapters in your textbook, so we'll summarize them here. Also remember that these are guidelines and not rules – organizations may not fit neatly into one or the other guideline because of the unique circumstances they face. The key point to remember is that *an organization needs to align its strategy, structure, design and culture with environmental characteristics and demands.*

1 In a stable environment a low-cost leadership or focus strategy is likely because they emphasize efficiency and control within a broad or narrow market. In this case a more mechanistic, functional or divisional structure will be appropriate: standardization, centralization, formal procedures, clear division of labour (differentiation) and close supervision. Cultural values of conformity, consistency, predictability, and routine are appropriate because little change is required – either a bureaucratic (efficiency) or mission (envisioning the future) culture. The UK's Civil Service, the US Federal and State Governments, and the Los Alamos National Laboratories are examples. These are organizations where government policies have to be implemented and applied in a regulated and consistent way.

2 In a dynamic, changing and unstable environment a differentiation or focus strategy might be more appropriate because they emphasize product/service development and innovation within a broad or narrow market. In this situation an organic or matrix structure will be appropriate: mutual adjustment, decentralized decision making, high integration (collaboration between departments), autonomy and creativity. A culture valuing flexibility and creativity is more appropriate – either a clan (involvement, teamwork) or adaptability (innovation) culture. For example, in a competitive high-tech environment, companies are often fighting to stay ahead and try to be proactive in looking for new products and creating new customer needs. A good example of this is Apple's introduction of the iPod – recall from section 3 that Apple's culture emphasizes risk-taking and being different.

Contemporary Approaches to Environment and Strategy

Weick's enacted environment

Karl Weick (1979) argues that although organizational strategy makers believe the environment is concrete with real elements and characteristics, those characteristics are constructed by strategy makers depending on how they perceive and interpret the environment (*social constructionism*). In other words, they *enact* (bring into being) the environment as they gather and analyse information. For example, if strategy makers perceive the environment as complex and uncertain, then they will set up systems to monitor what's happening, gather more data, develop more sophisticated forms of analysis and management – this will be self-confirming as they will enact a complex environment. Weick suggests that strategy involves improvisation, or a just-in-time approach in which events are interpreted and given meaning, and actions, conversations, memos, etc. create pieces of strategy.

Mintzberg's work on emergent strategy

Henry Mintzberg (1978, 1994) suggested that in reality, company strategies might not be as deliberate and planned as academics imply. He argues that strategy emerges over time in the intuitive understandings, actions and decisions made by various organizational members – and only later are these organized as the strategic plan. Strategy formulation is therefore not separate from strategy implementation – they occur simultaneously. Mintzberg believes that strategy should be both deliberate and emergent: deliberate because data collection and analysis allows the organization to anticipate and plan, emergent because this gives the organization flexibility to adapt to change.

Strategy as practice

One current field of interest is the notion of strategy as practice, which examines the everyday processes, practices, events and activities in organizations that relate to strategic outcomes. So the focus is on action and practice rather than planning models and techniques. Researchers carry out in-depth qualitative research to identify and examine strategizing practices and processes occurring at all levels of the organization, both deliberate and emergent.

INTEGRATIVE CASE

Let's look at how these ideas relate to our case. To recap:

You own and manage a restaurant in your local town, which seats up to 80 people, and is open for lunch and dinner. You serve an international cuisine, the price range of an entrée is moderate to high, and you offer elegant décor and a romantic atmosphere. You employ a staff of 30, including an Assistant Manager, chef and cooks, bar staff, waitpersons, cleaner and a cashier.

(Continued)

(Continued)

There is currently no real competition, with only a McDonald's and a Chinese restaurant in the town, but you hear rumours that there may be a new chain restaurant opening soon...

- Environmental complexity – pretty low, you operate in a specific locale with its own demographic characteristics. There are health regulations you will need to meet.
- Environmental stability – stable. This might change, for example if a new restaurant opens or if a major employer in town goes out of business, because these will affect your market. Competition may increase.
- Environmental richness – you have an available source of labour and a local college offering catering courses.
- Strategy – your strategy is a *focused differentiation* strategy because you want to remain in town, and you differentiate your restaurant from others by your menu and atmosphere. If competition increases, you might want to differentiate further by offering a range of organic or vegetarian dishes as part of your menu.
- Resource dependence – you are dependent on a local cut-price warehouse for your supplies. If you offer an organic or vegetarian menu you might approach a number of local growers for supplies (*multiple suppliers*).
- Institutional theory – your success depends on meeting the needs of your local customers, your financial backers and government regulations. Before opening your restaurant, you visited a number of restaurants in the region offering a similar cuisine, and discussed the operation and management with their owners. This gave you a number of ideas about how to manage your own restaurant (*mimetic isomorphism*).
- Life cycle – you are at the *creativity or entrepreneurial* stage of your organization's life cycle, and so you are going to be operating as an organic organization, learning how to address new problems and situations as they arise through mutual adjustment.

So look back at sections 1, 2 and 3 to see if you think there is an alignment between environment, strategy, structure, design and culture.

USING THE MATERIAL

Exam and discussion questions may relate to specific theories, or ask you a general question about the relationship between environment, strategy and structure. For example:

1   Using an organization of your choice, map out its organizational domain, the degree of uncertainty it might face, and how the organization tries to deal with environmental demands.

You might select an organization you work for, or select one from the Internet. Take each domain element, identify, for example, who the organization's suppliers, competitors and customers are. How uncertain is the environment based on complexity, richness and the degree of stability? How does the organization deal with demands through buffering and boundary-spanning activities, the type of structure (matrix, functional, organic, etc.) and the type of culture?

2   Explain the differences between Porter's three competitive strategies. Give examples of the type of organization (e.g. software design company, widget manufacturer) that might adopt each strategy and explain why the strategy would be appropriate.

This question assesses your understanding of Porter's model and its application. There are two ways of answering the question: (a) in three parts: describe the model, give examples of each strategy and then explain why; (b) take each strategy separately, describe one, give an example of an organization using this strategy, and explain why it is appropriate.

3   Why do organizations need to align their strategy, structure, design and culture with environmental characteristics and demands?

This is quite a difficult question because it requires you to bring in a number of different ideas and this may seem overwhelming. Stay focused. State why alignment is important – because environmental forces affect resource availability, competition, legitimacy, and therefore an organization's survival. Then explain how environment, strategy, structure, etc. are related (see the general guidelines throughout this section) and give examples. For example, you might want to discuss how more organic structures are appropriate for complex and unstable environments, and that organizational culture would need values and practices that support flexibility, innovation, autonomy and probably team work.

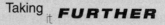

Taking it *FURTHER*

One of the issues that is becoming increasingly important in the field of environment, strategy and organization culture is that of sustainable development and corporate social responsibility. Sustainable development means making decisions, creating policies and practices that are not based solely on economic and financial considerations but also protect the environment and take into consideration social responsibilities. Socially responsible organizations make decisions that are ethical, protect and enhance the environment, engage in philanthropic activities such as investing in third world community development, contribute to charities and the arts, and provide benefits, training and development opportunities, and family-friendly practices for employees. It is argued that social responsibility improves the quality of life for all of us. Even though you will find that many organizations have a corporate social responsibility policy (usually on their website), some still resist or do the minimum to meet legal requirements. Why should organizations be socially responsible? What are some of the reasons for resisting social responsibility?

Textbook Guide

CHILD: *Chapters 2, 10 and 11.*
DAFT: *Chapters 2, 4, 5, 6 and 9.*
JONES: *Chapters 3, 8 and 11.*
WATSON: *Chapter 9.*

Additional Reading

Fernández-Alles, M. de la luz, and Valle-Cabrera, R. (2006) 'Reconciling institutional theory with organizational theories: how neoinstitutionalism resolves five paradoxes', *Journal of Organizational Change Management,* 4: 503–17.

Hodge, M. M. and Piccolo, R. F. (2005) 'Funding source, board involvement techniques, and financial vulnerability in nonprofit organizations: a test of resource dependence', *Nonprofit Management and Leadership,* 16: 171–90.

Lado, A. A., Boyd, N. G., Wright, P. and Kroll, M. (2006) 'Paradox and theorizing within the resource based view', *Academy of Management Review,* 31: 115–31.

Whittington, R. (2006) 'Completing the practice turn in strategy research', *Organization Studies,* 27: 613–34.

5

power, conflict and control

We now address the topics of power, conflict, and control. Each is part of everyday organizational life and therefore it's important to understand the ways in which power can be exercised effectively and appropriately, how to implement controls that measure performance but also motivate employees, and how to manage conflict effectively. Understanding the potential sources can help prevent organizational conflict. Your textbook may cover the three topics separately (e.g. Child, Daft and Jones have one chapter on conflict, power and politics, and a separate chapter on control), while others combine them (e.g., Hatch with Cunliffe). I have combined all three because they are interrelated:

- Power is associated with the ability to control resources and people.
- Conflict can result from struggles associated with various groups and individuals trying to gain control and power over others.

We will look at the main theories and issues in each, and then examine the interrelationship between them.

Definitions

- **Power** – when one person or group can influence another person or group to do something they might not otherwise do.
- **Organizational conflict** – when two or more groups and individuals compete or struggle to achieve their goals over others.
- **Control** – putting the mechanisms in place to ensure that performance meets the required goals and standards.

Power, Conflict and Control: Key Concepts

Power

You may remember from Part 1 that early work in organization theory (classical and scientific management) assumed that **power** is a manager's prerogative and is linked to formal authority and hierarchical level. **Control** is therefore an acceptable and legitimate aspect of a manager's position. Since then, a number of studies have suggested that power is more widely dispersed and has a number of sources (e.g., Crozier, 1964; Hickson et al., 1971; Pfeffer, 1981). Many of these sources relate to having something that makes other people dependent on you – it's this dependency that gives you power. These sources may include:

- Formal – Legitimate power based on job title, position in hierarchy, defined authority and control over decision making.
- Personal – Based on a person's charisma and personality.
- Expertise – A person or department has expertise needed by the organization.
- Knowledge – A person or department has knowledge needed by the organization.
- Resource – A person or department controls resources needed by others.
- Reward – A person has the ability to reward performance.
- Coercive – A person has the ability to apply sanctions or punishment.
- Information – Having access to, and an ability to collect, analyse and use information for decision making and control purposes.
- Centrality – A person has a key position in the organizational network: is able to control resources, space, budgets; has a central physical location; or is doing work that is relevant to and impacts organizational goals.
- Visibility – Performance can be seen by others.
- Referent – People are influenced by identification, admiration and the need to seek approval.
- Track record – Success in performance.
- Symbolic management – An ability to move people emotionally through powerful language, ceremonies and artifacts.

Strategic contingencies theory develops the notion that power can be exercised in a number of ways by a number of sources. For example, Hickson and colleagues (1971) suggested that power is based on the ability of an individual or department to solve critical organizational problems and help the organization deal with uncertainty. Pfeffer (1981) suggested that power can also be based on having a skill needed by others or having access to scarce resources. For example, if the organization faces a lawsuit for sexual harassment, the Human Resource Management Department has the knowledge and expertise to help the organization deal with the issue and prevent further lawsuits. So they might gain resources – additional staffing and finance – to help them do so ... which gives the HR Department more power if they are able to hang on to these resources. For Pfeffer this is a way of adapting to environmental demands, but power can extend beyond its original use as those with power hang on to it.

As you may have experienced, or realize through your reading, power is also associated with **politics** – activities designed to increase one's power and control over others. Politics can be both negative in the sense that they are self-serving and time-wasting, but can be positive if it is the means by which knowledge and expertise are geared towards improving organizational effectiveness.

Organizational politics can be seen in various strategies for increasing and developing power. These include:

- Creating dependencies by holding resources and developing knowledge and expertise needed by others.
- Controling access to and the flow of information (centrality).
- Controling agendas and influencing decision-making criteria.
- Building coalitions with other individuals and departments.
- Placing yourself on key committees and decision-making bodies.
- Working on building a variety of sources of power.

Organizational conflict

Conflict is inevitable in organizations because various stakeholders have different goals: shareholders to maximize profits, accountants to measure and control costs, employees to do interesting work and/or maximize their pay, etc. Most textbooks agree that conflict can be both counterproductive in terms of deflecting effort from goals and – if managed effectively – beneficial in leading to creativity and change. From a manager's perspective it's important to be able to anticipate the potential for conflict, understand how to avoid it and recognize when conflict can lead to change. One of the most well-known models of **organizational conflict**, and the one covered in most OT textbooks, is Pondy's (1967) five stage model:

The key is to recognize conflict at each stage, and manage it appropriately.

Potential sources of conflict include a number of structural and design issues:

1 *Differing goals*: different departments may have different goals e.g., production want long continuous product runs because they are efficient; sales want to meet individual customer needs.

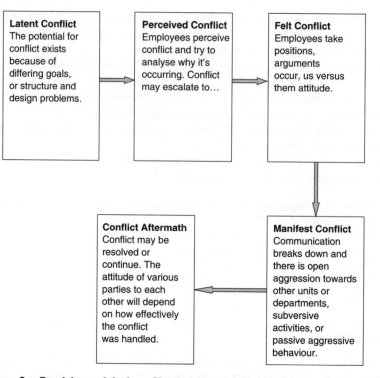

Latent Conflict
The potential for conflict exists because of differing goals, or structure and design problems.

Perceived Conflict
Employees perceive conflict and try to analyse why it's occurring. Conflict may escalate to...

Felt Conflict
Employees take positions, arguments occur, us versus them attitude.

Conflict Aftermath
Conflict may be resolved or continue. The attitude of various parties to each other will depend on how effectively the conflict was handled.

Manifest Conflict
Communication breaks down and there is open aggression towards other units or departments, subversive activities, or passive aggressive behaviour.

Figure 6   Pondy's model of conflict (1967) from 'Organization Conflict: Concepts and Models' by Louis R. Pondy, *Administrative Science Quarterly*, Vol. 12, September 1967. Copyright © Administrative Science Quarterly.

2 *Differentiation*: both vertical and horizontal. Senior managers are concerned with organization-wide issues, professional and technical employees with their own department issues and interests. Departments develop their own goals and norms that may be in conflict with other departments (recall Lawrence and Lorsch (1967), section 4).

3 *Task interdependence*: when departments depend on others to achieve their goals, the potential for conflict exists (recall Thompson's (1967) model of interdependence in section 2).

4 *Poor integration*: adequate and appropriate integrating mechanisms may not exist to minimize and address conflicting goals, poor communication and a lack of cooperation between levels and departments.

5 *Scarce resources*: departments may fight over money, physical and staff resources.

6 *Individual differences*: gender, age, race, personality, goals, etc.

7 *Incompatible rewards*: the reward system does not match performance expectations, e.g., employees are required to work as a
team to achieve team goals, but receive bonuses based on individual
performance.

8 *Unclear responsibilities*: when goals, roles and responsibilities
are not clarified and formalized.

Managing conflict means:

- Evaluating organizational design and structure to identify and eliminate poten-
tial sources of conflict (catch conflict at the 'latent' stage).
- Clarifying department goals, roles, responsibilities, as well as emphasizing
how these relate to common organizational goals.
- Establishing integrating mechanisms to encourage collaboration (see section 1).
- Have a system for dealing with conflict to try to prevent escalation (e.g., griev-
ance procedure, dispute resolution, mediators, and so on).
- Deal with conflict in a timely manner, in the early stages rather than the later ones.

Control

Much of what we have covered up to this point is about control in one
form or another. Organization structure, design and technology is about
controlling work, resources and information; organizational culture is about
controlling the behaviour and actions of people; organizations want to
increase their control over the environment by developing an effective strategy and ways of managing environmental demands (e.g., resource dependence, boundary spanning and buffering activities). Consequently, control
is covered in different chapters in different textbooks: Child in Control, Daft
in Information Technology and Control, Hatch with Cunliffe in
Organizational Power, Control and Conflict, Jones in Organization
Structure: Authority and Control, and Watson in Organizational Structure,
Culture and Change. You will need to understand the key concepts, but also
make sure you know the emphasis your textbook and instructor place on
control – where do they see control fitting?

It's important to remember there are different types of control:

1 *Strategic control*: of an organization's resources, markets and
other environmental sectors. This may include establishing and
revaluating performance measures (metrics) related to the strategic

plan, setting dashboard measures – key indicators of organizational performance, the balanced scorecard which includes key financial, operational (internal processes), customer service, and learning and growth measures, benchmarking the organization's performance compared with competitors and other successful organizations.

2 *Operational control*: control over work and performance.

3 *Output controls*: measure results and outcomes such as production goals, sales goals, quality standards, scrap rates, and customer complaints. These can be used where it is possible to measure results. A hospital can measure bed utilization, patient throughflow, drug costs etc., all output controls – but do these give a measure of patient care and satisfaction? To get a fuller picture, the hospital might also need to consider:

4 *Behavioural controls*: measure effective behaviours such as patient care, responsiveness to customers, collaboration with other departments etc. These are used where outputs cannot be measured or only give a limited view.

5 *Bureaucratic controls*: Ouchi (1979) suggested the next three types of control as forms of control through cooperation. Bureaucratic controls include defining and monitoring tasks, goals, job descriptions, responsibilities, rules and procedures, and output goals, etc., through close supervision. Government organizations often use bureaucratic controls.

6 *Market controls*: based on the idea that efficiency is related to an organization's ability to remain price competitive. The revenues and costs of the organization, profit centre/division, and/or department are identified and compared with past performance, competitors, other divisions and departments. Local authorities in the UK, and city governments in the US, opened up services such as refuse collection, transportation, road maintenance, information technology systems to bid, thus using price competition as a way of controlling costs.

7 *Clan control*: clan control is a form of control through organizational culture because it's based on socializing organizational members into commitment to the organization's mission, vision, values and norms, perhaps through autonomy and teamwork.

You also need to be aware of two theories of control: Agency theory and the Cybernetic model.

Agency theory is based on the idea that owners and shareholders (principals) are dependent on managers and other employees (agents) to achieve company goals. This is risky because the principal needs to make sure that agents will use their knowledge and expertise to act in the best interest of the company and not their own self-interest – known as the *agency problem*. Various mechanisms can be used to control the behaviour of agents, including contracts, performance measures, stock options, information systems, and linking rewards to specific outputs.

The *cybernetic model* of control takes a systems approach to suggest that organizational and individual goals can be aligned if goals and standards are set, feedback mechanisms are established to compare performance against goals (performance measures, performance evaluation systems, etc.), and then adjustments are made depending on the result. Positive results are rewarded, negative results punished, or the goal may be adjusted.

Contemporary Approaches to Power, Conflict and Control

Contemporary approaches often deal with power, control and conflict as interrelated issues, that in practice are difficult to separate. Note this relationship as I outline a number of approaches below.

Critical theory

Based on the work of Karl Marx, critical theorists claim that power and control are embedded in social, political and economic structures and practices, and that this results in the domination and exploitation of groups by capitalist interests. Critical theorists challenge managerial ideologies with the aim of emancipating dominated groups through more democratic modes of governance and management. Some of the main concepts are:

- *Ideology*: a particular set of values, beliefs and practices that favour one group (e.g., owners, shareholders, managers) over another (workers).
- **Hegemony**: groups comply with their domination because it's an accepted part of life, e.g., I have autonomy in my job, so I believe I've been given freedom to do what I want – whereas it's another way of getting more work out of me and therefore benefiting managers and shareholders.
- *Labour process theory*: Work is deskilled (simplified and routinized) so that work and workers can be easily controlled. Cheap low-skilled workers can be hired and easily replaced if they create resistance or conflict.
- *Systematically distorted communication*: when power and control are exercised by emphasizing one meaning and ideology over others. For example, when efficiency is pushed at the expense of worker concerns.

Postmodern approaches

Based on Foucault's idea of **disciplinary power** existing in everyday practices and relationships, organization theorists study how such power exists in organizations. For example, training, performance evaluations, group norms, operating procedures, interactions between managers and employees and between team members, are all forms of disciplinary power because they control our actions, behaviour, identity and our bodies. Disciplinary power also relates to **self-surveillance**, when employees monitor their own behaviour and comply with organizational goals because of a system that causes them to do so. For example, if you have a performance management system at work you probably have annual goals that you have identified with your manager. You monitor your performance over the year and make sure you are doing the right tasks to achieve those goals – because your pay raise depends on it.

INTEGRATIVE CASE

Let's look at the various sources of power and control that you might use in your restaurant. Remember:

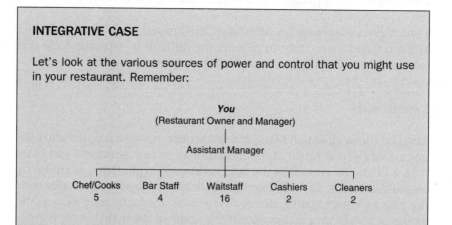

You
(Restaurant Owner and Manager)

Assistant Manager

| Chef/Cooks | Bar Staff | Waitstaff | Cashiers | Cleaners |
| 5 | 4 | 16 | 2 | 2 |

As the restaurant owner and manager, you have a number of different sources of power: formal, reward, coercive, knowledge about restaurant management, centrality and maybe more! What are these based on and what additional sources may you draw on?

Your Assistant Manager will also have formal power, perhaps with knowledge and expertise. Your Chef also has power, perhaps based on expertise, centrality (she or he cooks the food that has a direct impact on customer satisfaction!) and probably a track record. The bar staff have knowledge and expertise in alcohol and the mixing of drinks. Do you

(Continued)

think the waitstaff, cashiers and cleaning staff have any sources of power?

You are also the principal (owner) dependant on the agents (Assistant Manager, Chef, etc.) to achieve your goals. So what forms of control might you consider? You are a small organization, with limited resources, so your controls might include:

- Operational – measures for how employees perform their work and achieve their goals.
- Output – e.g., clear goals for each type of job, the timely processing of orders, minimum food wastage and customer satisfaction.
- Behavioural – e.g., waitstaff demonstrate courtesy, an ability to work with other employees, promptness.
- Bureaucratic – e.g., compliance with hygiene regulations, budgetary controls, direct supervision.
- Clan – e.g., activities and interaction that help employees identify with organizational goals, collaboration and mutual support.

How might you balance the benefits and disadvantages of conflict? How might you minimize the potential for negative conflict?

USING THE MATERIAL

1 Discuss the benefits and drawbacks to an organization of conflict and political behaviour.

Most textbooks will talk about the advantages and disadvantages of conflict. Discuss these, giving examples if you can, and then talk about the importance of building on the advantages of conflict, managing conflict to prevent negative impacts (recall the Pondy model). Regarding political behaviour, while it can result in wasted time and effort and lead to conflict, the strategic contingency model suggests that it is a way of aligning knowledge and expertise with critical problems and issues. The key is not allowing one group or department to keep its power and resources when the issue has been resolved. Power needs to shift depending on the problems that need resolving.

2 Explain the relationship between organizational conflict, organization structure and organizational design?

See the section on 'Organizational conflict'. Give examples.

Taking it *FURTHER*

How might greater decentralization, autonomy and self-managed work teams impact the agency *problem*? Remember the problem is how to control the behaviour of employees who often have greater knowledge in a specific area than a principal. Are performance management systems and 360 degree appraisal systems possible control mechanisms?

Textbook Guide

CHILD: *Chapter 5.*
DAFT: *Chapters 8 and 13.*
JONES: *Chapters 5 and 14.*
HATCH WITH CUNLIFFE: *Chapter 8.*
WATSON: *Chapters 2 and 6.*

Additional Reading

Deetz, S. A. (1992) 'Disciplinary power in the modern corporation', in M. Alvesson and H. Wilmott (eds), *Critical Management Studies.* London: Sage. pp. 21–45.

Foucault, M. (1980) *Power/Knowledge: Selected Interviews and Other Writings by Michel Foucault, 1972–1977.* (ed. C. Gordon) New York: Pantheon.

Martin, J., Knopoff, K. and Beckman, C. (1998) 'An alternative to bureaucratic impersonality and emotional labor: bounded emotionality at the Body Shop', *Administrative Science Quarterly,* 43: 429–69.

Sewell, G. (1998) 'The discipline of teams: the control of team-based industrial work through electronic and peer surveillance', *Administrative Science Quarterly,* 43: 397–429.

6

innovation, change and organizational learning

Every OT textbook covers change and innovation, often in a separate chapter (e.g. Child, Daft, Jones) or combined with **organizational learning** (Hatch with Cunliffe). Change happens continually through employee turnover, new technology, new product or service development, and changing environmental demands. Think about some of the current fads or methods that have been introduced in many organizations over the last 20 years: keiretsu, business process reengineering (BPR), total quality management (TQM), quality circles, kanban, flexible/self-managed work teams, balanced scorecards, etc. You will find all of these mentioned somewhere in your book – and all involved introducing change. In addition, remember the organizational life cycle model from section 4? Well, this model assumes that organizations grow and this involves changes in size, structure and culture. Innovation in the form of new products/services, technologies, equipment and work processes, is necessary if an organization is to compete, and is therefore an essential part of change. And organizational learning relates to how organizations capture, create and use knowledge to help them adapt to change. You will need to understand why change, innovation and organizational learning are important, various forms and types, and strategies for managing each.

Definitions

- **Innovation**: developing new products, services, technology, work processes, markets, and organizational structures and designs.
- **Organizational change**: moving from a current to a desired state. May be **revolutionary** or **evolutionary, planned** or **emergent, radical** or **incremental** (see Glossary for definitions and examples).
- *Organizational learning*: improving the organization's, teams' and individual employee's ability to acquire and create new knowledge in order to improve organizational performance.

Key Concepts

Innovation

Think about innovation as a deliberate strategy for change, because it involves developing (or buying) new products and processes as a means of making the organization more competitive, effective and efficient. This obviously will mean making changes – not just in terms of introducing new products or technology, but making old ones obsolete. Innovation can be crucial in helping an organization manage or respond to changes in its environment. Your textbook might talk about *entrepreneurs* who start new businesses, and *intrapreneurs,* employees who develop new ideas and manage the development process in an organization. In the US, *skunk works* is a fairly common term used to describe temporary teams of employees created to promote innovation. Some organizations have a reputation for innovation (e.g., Virgin, IKEA, Honda). A Boston Consulting Group 2006 survey of 'The World's Most Innovative Companies' lists Apple, Google, 3M, Toyota and Microsoft as the top five innovative companies. Innovation can be crucial in creating and maintaining an organization's competitive advantage, as well as contributing to economic growth generally.

Some of the key concepts you will probably need to know include the various types of innovation, and how innovation relates to organization structure and culture. Types of innovation include:

- Process innovation: developments in the production process and the way products or services are produced, including equipment, work methods, materials and work systems. The drive for process innovation is usually cost effectiveness.
- Product innovation: the introduction of new products or services, or variations of existing products and services. The drive for product innovation is often to increase market share, meet customer demands, and/or improve quality. In this case there is a definite outcome to innovation in that new products are available. The iPod is a good example of product innovation.
- Technical innovation: changes in the technology associated with the work process or service. The drive for technical innovation is usually increasing efficiency.
- Administrative innovation: innovations in organization structure, strategy and administrative processes. The drive is often based on a need to become more efficient, effective and flexible in meeting customer needs.

It's important to remember that the organization structure, design and culture need to encourage and support innovation, creativity and risk taking. This means a more organic structure with design factors including: decentralization, mutual adjustment, low formalization, and probably high integration, and an organizational culture that is flexible, and supports risk-taking, collaboration and initiative. 3M is a good example of an organization that encourages and supports innovation through intrapreneurship. They have a seven-point list covering what it takes to be innovative:[1]

1 Show a commitment to innovation by providing support, e.g., financial support and making time available to work on ideas. 3M spends about seven percent of sales on research.

2 Maintain an innovative culture through hiring, stories, encouraging risk-taking and tolerating mistakes. When a new product reaches particular sales targets, a new department and then a business unit is created. The business unit operates as a profit centre.

3 Have a broad range of technologies so that ideas from one can be used in others, e.g., a layered plastic lens technology was used in the development of golf gloves that give a tighter grip.

4 Create opportunities for talk and networking between researchers to encourage idea generation. 3M has 'technology forums' where researchers present papers and discuss projects.

5 Set expectations and reward people for outstanding work. There are awards, salary raises and promotions for employees who innovate and make a major contribution to the business.

6 Evaluate and quantify the success of innovations.

7 Base research on customer needs. Customers participate in generating ideas.

These points are embedded in 3M's structure and culture.

Organizational change

Change may not necessarily involve innovation in the sense of new products and processes (i.e., radical change), but modifications to existing ways of doing things on a more incremental level. Most textbooks talk about the issues and demands – the forces – that can lead to organizational change. Managers need to monitor these and be aware of when change is needed. Figure 7 summarises the main forces.

You should note that while many are external, environmental forces, there can also be internal forces for change (problems, leadership changes, innovation and changes that emerge as employees do their work).

When implementing changes at an organizational, group or individual level, managers need to think about why change might be resisted. Lewin's *Force Field Theory* (1951) is often cited as a way of analysing resistance – that there are always forces for change and against change at work in an organization. Managers need to identify these, minimize resisting forces and build on driving forces as a means of facilitating change. Change can be resisted for many reasons, including: reduced power and status of groups and individuals, loyalty to a particular department or unit, a formal bureaucratic structure (specific jobs, rules, procedures), organization culture (values, norms, accepted practices), break up of work groups, individual and group processes (norms, routines, insecurity, no buy in to the goal of the change), and so on. The forces for change include those in Figure 7, as well as such things as an organic structure, change increasing power or status, making work easier, or resulting in increased pay and benefits through greater efficiency. Lewin suggests that change involves:

1 *Unfreezing* the organization by creating the need for change, unsettling established practices and overcoming resistance.

2 *Movement*, implementing the change through new structures, systems, procedures, management styles and training.

3 *Refreezing* which ensures changes are adhered to.

Your textbook will identify various strategies for managing change. These might include:

1 *Kotter's eight-stage model (1996)*: establish a sense of urgency, create guiding coalitions, develop a vision and strategy, communicate the vision, empower employees, create short-term wins, consolidate changes, link the change to new cultural values and practices.

2 *A change strategy*: (a) Identify problems, need and/or opportunities for change; (b) Gather information about the change and who will be affected, consult; (c) Anticipate resistance (force field

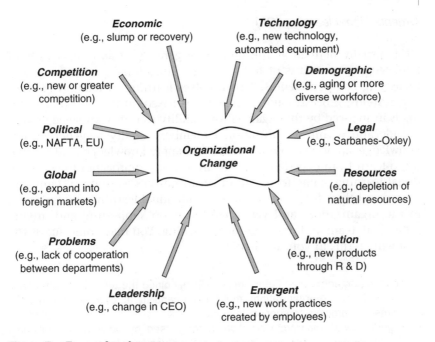

Economic
(e.g., slump or recovery)

Technology
(e.g., new technology,
automated equipment)

Competition
(e.g., new or greater
competition)

Demographic
(e.g., aging or more
diverse workforce)

Political
(e.g., NAFTA, EU)

Legal
(e.g., Sarbanes-Oxley)

**Organizational
Change**

Global
(e.g., expand into
foreign markets)

Resources
(e.g., depletion of
natural resources)

Problems
(e.g., lack of cooperation
between departments)

Innovation
(e.g., new products
through R & D)

Leadership
(e.g., change in CEO)

Emergent
(e.g., new work practices
created by employees)

Figure 7   Forces for change

analysis); (d) Plan the change, ensuring you have the necessary resources and support; (e) Implement the change with flexibility to meet unanticipated consequences; and (f) evaluate success.

3 *Organizational development*: a planned, long-term, organization-wide process of changing structure, culture, systems and processes using ideas from the behavioural sciences. This usually means introducing more flexible and/or team-based structures, and involves employees in the process of identifying problems and solutions, and managing and implementing changes. Techniques such as process consulting, sensitivity training, and team building are used. It can also involve:

4 *Action research*: bringing in consultants to help organizational members diagnose organizational problems by gathering and evaluating data (e.g., surveys), and by developing and implementing solutions.

5 *Cultural change*: Redefining the organization's goals, mission, vision, values, and changing the stories and heroes.

Organizational learning (OL)

OL is usually defined as the process of generating and applying new knowledge as a means of improving organizational performance and increasing competitiveness. This involves learning in relation to strategy, systems, processes and people. OL is based on the idea that learning is influenced by the organization's ability to utilize knowledge from outside and within; organizational members' ability to generate new knowledge; an ability to understand and apply knowledge; and an ability to learn from experience. There are various approaches to organizational learning, some focus on an organization's learning systems and processes, others focus on developing individual learning and linking it to the organization, and yet others focus on supporting and linking individual, team and organizational learning. You may come across the following terms in your textbook:

- *Learning organizations:* Peter Senge (1990) coined the term 'learning organization' for those organizations that have a capacity to learn and the mechanisms and process to support learning.
- *Organizational knowledge creation:* a term used by Nonaka and Takeuchi (1995) for the process by which organizations use knowledge and innovations created by individuals.
- **Knowledge management**: relates to systems and methods used to share knowledge and expertise throughout the organization. It's often associated with codifying knowledge and information using information technology and information systems, but is seen to be part of the organizational learning process.
- *Communities of Practice:* Lave and Wenger (1991) suggested that learning occurs in practice. People construct their understanding as they do their work and interact with others. So learning often takes place in a community (of work colleagues, classmates, an orchestra, nurses, etc.) as we learn to become community members. They emphasized that learning takes place *in* practice (not *from* practice) in informal and social ways. Some organizations have developed Communities of Practice (CoPs), which are informal groups of employees working on areas and projects of mutual interest. IBM, British Petroleum and Xerox are examples of companies supporting CoPs.

You should also be familiar with the following ideas:

1 *March's two modes of OL* (1991): *Exploration* is when organizational members search for and experiment with new procedures, processes, ways of thinking and acting. For example, the organization might change from a functional structure to the use of autonomous

work teams. *Exploitation* is the modification and use of existing knowledge and systems in more efficient and effective ways. For example, changes might be made to standard operating procedures in a manufacturing plant to increase efficiency.

2 *Polanyi's two types of knowledge* (1966): *Explicit* knowledge is that which is articulated, formalized and codified in policy, procedure and operating manuals. *Tacit* knowledge is the intuitive and personal knowledge that we do not, or cannot, articulate but it helps us do our jobs competently. A key issue in OL is how to transform tacit to explicit knowledge.

3 *Argyris and Schön's single and double-loop learning* (1978): Organizations need to incorporate two forms of learning to increase their effectiveness. *Single-loop* learning is a form of problem solving; it involves learning by reflecting on how problems were handled and then applying that knowledge to avoid similar problems. *Double-loop* learning involves questioning assumptions, ways of thinking, values and actions to think about strategies and issues in new ways. (Note, this is akin to exploration.)

Contemporary Approaches

Organizations emerging in social processes

A contemporary approach to organizational change is based on the idea that change is not something that happens to disrupt the normal way of working in organizations, but is part of everyday organizational life. In other words, the models of change, summarized earlier in the section, assume that organizational stability is the norm and that change needs to be managed. If you recollect structuration theory and the idea of routines and improvisations that we discussed in sections 1 and 2, then you will begin to see that change is ongoing. Tsoukas and Chia (2002) elaborated this idea, arguing that change is ongoing and that organizations are always *'becoming'*, because organizational members continually adapt and modify their actions as they go about their work. So organizations are not entities, but unfolding processes of actions, events, choices, behaviours and so on. The implications are that managers need to recognize when to build on these unfolding processes and perhaps expand them across the organization.

Two additional ways of implementing change include:

Appreciative Inquiry (AI)

AI supports learning from successes and strengths by focusing on what works well in the organization and then building on that. It utilizes collaborative and inclusive approaches to change management.

Steps in the AI process:

1 Interview people to find out what works well.

2 Identify common themes.

3 Articulate propositions – envision possibilities.

4 Validate propositions through action. Mechanisms are needed in the organization.

5 Develop an action agenda and create commitments.

6 Implement – action planning.

7 Evaluation.

Future search conferences

Search conferencing is used particularly in the public sector in the US where community planning is important. It is a participatory approach to planning and design and incorporates a need for all participants (administrators, politicians, community members) to learn in the process. Usually, a large group of people (20–30, 70) meet in a retreat setting. A planning group has already identified the problem. Participants at the search conference then:

- share views of the history
- Collectively identify problems
- create action plans to resolve the problems
- choose an action plan.

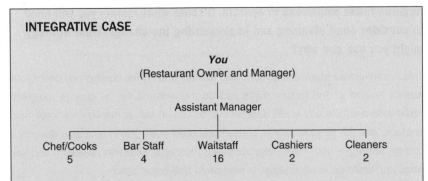

INTEGRATIVE CASE

As a fairly new organization in it's creativity or entrepreneurial stage of growth, you are probably not going to make any major changes, and at this stage you might be concerned with March's idea of *exploitation* of knowledge, but are not big enough to need knowledge management systems. And unless you create a new dish or cooking technique, you are probably not going to spend a lot of time and effort on innovation. But if you do make changes, Lewin's force field analysis will be helpful in thinking about how to anticipate resistance and manage the change process. Many of the ideas and techniques discussed here are more appropriate for medium to large-sized organizations where knowledge and learning need to be more formalized and systematic, and resources are available to create a learning organization and OD initiatives.

USING THE MATERIAL

1   What are the forces for, and barriers to organizational change, and why do managers need to understand these?

In answering this question you need to think about the macro forces (Figure 7) and also some of the internal forces (Lewin's force field analysis). You could even use the force field analysis format to identify the forces for and against, and then explain them.

2   You are the Production Manager in XYZ, and you are introducing new automated equipment that will increase productivity, decrease scrap and

requires fewer employees to operate. Discuss what factors you will need to consider when planning and implementing the change. What strategy might you use and why?

This is a mini case study and so you need to bear in mind the context and orient your answer around it. The factors might include the reasons for the change, possible resistance and how you would deal with it. You could talk about Lewin's force field analysis, and the need to inform, consult and build trust. You should also discuss a change strategy – you might select one (e.g., Kotter's, or action research) and say what you would do at each stage in relation to this organization.

3   How can managers develop organizational learning

Review the approaches and techniques covered in your textbook. You can talk about how to develop and link learning between individual, team and organizational levels. You might also want to talk about the role of CoPs and give examples of organizations using these practices.

Taking it **FURTHER**

So far we've talked about innovation, change and learning within organizations. Do you think that this does, can or should occur between organizations? What might encourage and discourage learning alliances between organizations? The need for an organization to retain its competitive advantage is obviously a force against sharing information and knowledge, but why and how might strategic alliances and joint ventures lead to a need for a learning alliance or knowledge sharing?

Note

1 From *Business Week*, 10 May, 2006. 3M's Seven Pillars of Innovation. M. Arendt. http://www.businessweek.com/innovate/content/may2006/id 20060510_682823.htm, accessed May 1, 2007.

Textbook Guide

CHILD: *Chapters 12 and 13.*
DAFT: *Chapter 11.*
HATCH WITH CUNLIFFE: *Chapter 9.*
JONES: *Chapters 10, 12 and 13.*
WATSON: *Chapter 7.*

Additional Reading

Cook, S. and Yanow, D. (1993) 'Culture and organizational learning', *Journal of Management Inquiry,* 7: 373–90.

Damanpour, F. and Aravind, D. (2006) 'Product and process innovation: a review of organizational and environmental determinants', in J. Hage and M. Meeus (eds), *Innovation, Science, and Institutional Change.* Oxford, New York: Oxford University Press.

Hargrave, T. J. and Van de Ven, A. H. (2006) 'A Collective action model of institutional innovation', *Academy of Management Review,* 31: 864–88.

Kanter, R. M., Stein, B. A. and Jick, T. D. (1992) *The Challenge of Organizational Change: How Companies Experience it and Leaders Guide it.* New York: Free Press.

Sampson, R. C. (2007) 'R & D alliances and firm performance: the impact of technological diversity and alliance organization on innovation', *Academy of Management Journal,* 50: 364–86.

Tsoukas, H. and Chia, R. (2002) 'On organizational becoming: rethinking organizational change', *Organization Science,* 13: 567–85.

part three

study, writing and revision skills

If you work your way carefully through this Part of the book, you should be better equipped to profit from your lectures, benefit from your seminars, construct your essays efficiently, develop effective revision strategies and respond comprehensively to the pressures of exam situations. In the six sections that lie ahead you will be presented with:

- checklists and bullet points to focus your attention on key issues
- exercises to help you participate actively in the learning experience
- illustrations and analogies to enable you to anchor learning principles in everyday events and experiences
- worked examples to demonstrate the use of such features as structure, headings and continuity
- tips that provide practical advice in nutshell form.

In the exercises that are presented, each student should decide how much effort they would like to invest in each exercise, according to individual preferences and requirements. Some of the points in the exercises will be covered in the text either before or after the exercise. You might prefer to read each section right through before going back to tackle the exercises. Suggested answers are provided in italics after some of the exercises, so avoid these if you prefer to work through the exercises on your own. The aim is to prompt you to reflect on the material, remember what you have read and trigger you to add your own thoughts. Space is provided for you to write your responses down in a few words, or you may prefer to reflect on them within your own mind. However, writing will help you to slow down and digest the material and may also enable you to process the information at a deeper level of learning.

Finally the overall aim of this Part of the book is to point you to the keys for academic and personal development. The twin emphases of academic development and personal qualities are stressed throughout. By giving attention to these factors you will give yourself the toolkit you will need to excel in your studies.

1	
how to get the most out of your lectures	

This section will show you how to.

- Make the most of your lecture notes
- Prepare your mind for new terminology
- Develop an independent approach to learning
- Write efficient summary notes from lectures
- Take the initiative in building on your lectures.

Keeping in Context

Learning is facilitated when it is set within an overall learning context, and it is the responsibility of your tutors to provide this context, for example, introducing you to the scope of OT and why it's important. However, it is your responsibility to ensure you understand this overall context by becoming familiar with the outline content of both a given subject and the entire study programme. You can do this before your course begins by reviewing the textbook and Part 1 in your course companion, this helps to think about where each topic fits into the overall scheme of things before you go into each lecture. Think, for example, of how confident you feel when you move into a new city (e.g. to attend university) once you become familiar with your surroundings – i.e. where you live in relation to college, shops, stores, buses, trains, places of entertainment, etc.

> *The same principle applies to your course – find your way around your study programme and locate the position of each lecture within this overall framework.*

Use of Lecture Notes

It is always beneficial to do some preliminary reading before you enter a lecture. If lecture notes are provided in advance (e.g. electronically), then print these out, read them, read your textbook and this book (see Part 1), make notes, and bring them to the lecture. You can insert question marks on issues where you will need further clarification. Some lecturers prefer to provide full notes, some prefer to make skeleton outlines available and some prefer to issue no notes at all! If notes are provided, take full advantage and supplement these with your own notes as you read the book and participate in class. In a later section on memory techniques you see that humans possess an ability for 're-learning savings' – i.e. it is easier to learn material the second time round, as it is evident that we have a capacity to hold residual memory deposits. So some basic preparation will equip you with a great advantage – you will be able to 'tune in' and think more clearly about the lecture.

> *If you set yourself too many tedious tasks at the early stages of your academic programme you may lose some motivation and momentum. A series of short, simple, achievable tasks can give your mind the 'lubrication' you need. For example, you are more likely to maintain preliminary reading for a lecture if you set modest targets.*

Mastering Technical Terms

OT contains many terms that may be new to you, such as 'paradigm', 'differentiation' and 'social constructionism'. These can be difficult to grasp and can make lectures confusing when you are trying to remember what they mean. But stick with it – there is a Glossary on p. 165 you should find helpful, and as you work through the course and come across the words again, you will find they will begin to make sense. It's also helpful to think of practical examples of theories because they can help put an abstract term into a practical context. Remember also that people learn differently: some learn visually, some by talking through ideas with a study group, others by writing key concepts. As a student I found I could recall information more effectively by writing definitions and theories on index cards that I could refer to quickly when needed. Figure out what's best for you, but remember that you will probably come across a range of teaching techniques, lectures, group discussions and projects, case studies, etc., and so it's best to try developing different approaches to learning. The checklist below may be of some help in mastering and marshalling the terms you hear in lectures.

Checklist – mastering terms used in your lectures

✓ Read lecture notes before the lectures and list any unfamiliar terms

✓ Read over the listed terms until you are familiar with them

✓ Try to work out meanings of terms from their context

✓ Do not suspend learning the meaning of a term indefinitely

✓ Write out a sentence that includes the new word (do this for each word)

✓ Meet with other students and test each other with the technical terms

✓ Jot down new words you hear in lectures and check out the meaning soon afterwards

Your confidence will greatly increase when you begin to follow the flow of arguments that contain technical terms, and more especially when you can freely use the terms yourself in speaking and writing.

Developing Independent Study

In the current educational ethos there are the twin aims of cultivating teamwork/group activities and independent learning. There is not necessarily a conflict between the two, they should complement each other. For example, if you are committed to independent learning you have more to offer other students when you work in small groups, and you will also be prompted to follow up on the leads given by them. Furthermore, the guidelines given to you in lectures are designed to lead you into deeper independent study. The issues raised in lectures are pointers to provide direction and structure for your extended personal pursuit. Your aim should invariably be to build on what you are given, and you should never think of merely returning the bare bones of the lecture material in a coursework essay or exam.

It is always very refreshing to a marker to be given work from a student that contains recent studies that the examiner had not previously encountered.

Note-taking Strategy

Note taking in lectures is an art that you will only perfect with practice and by trial and error. Each student should find the formula that works best for him or her. What works for one, does not work for the other.

Some students can write more quickly than others, some are better at shorthand than others and some are better at deciphering their own scrawl! The problem will always be to try to find a balance between concentrating beneficially on what you hear, with making sufficient notes that will enable you to comprehend later what you have heard. You should not, however, become frustrated by the fact that you will not understand or remember immediately everything you have heard.

> *By being present at a lecture, and by making some attempt to attend to what you hear, you will already have a substantial advantage over those students who do not attend.*

Checklist – note taking in lectures

✓ Develop the note-taking strategy that works best for you

✓ Work at finding a balance between listening and writing

✓ Make some use of optimal shorthand (e.g. a few key words may summarize a story)

✓ Too much writing may impair the flow of the lecture for you

✓ Too much writing may impair the quality of your notes

✓ Some limited notes are better than none

✓ Good note taking may facilitate deeper processing of information

✓ It is essential to 'tidy up' notes as soon as possible after a lecture

✓ Reading over notes soon after lectures will consolidate your learning

Developing the Lecture

Some educationalists have criticized the value of lectures because they allege that these are a mode of merely 'passive learning'. This can certainly be an accurate conclusion to arrive at (that is, if students approach lectures in the wrong way) and lecturers can work to devise ways of making lectures more interactive. For example, they can make use of interactive handouts or by posing questions during the lecture and giving time out for students to reflect on these. Other possibilities are short discussions at given junctures in the lecture or use of small groups within the session. As a student you do not have to enter a lecture in passive mode and you can ensure that you are not merely a passive recipient of information by taking steps to develop the lecture yourself. A list of suggestions is presented below to help you take the initiative in developing the lecture content.

Checklist – getting the most from lectures

✓ Try to interact with the lecture material by asking questions

✓ Highlight points that you would like to develop in personal study

✓ Trace connections between the lecture and other parts of your study programme

✓ Bring together notes from the lecture and other sources

✓ Restructure the lecture outline into your own preferred format

✓ Think of ways in which aspects of the lecture material can be applied

✓ Design ways in which aspects of the lecture material can be illustrated

✓ If the lecturer invites questions, make a note of all the questions asked

✓ Follow up on issues of interest that have arisen out of the lecture

You can contribute to this active involvement in a lecture by engaging with the material before, during and after it is delivered.

2

how to make the most of your seminars

This section will help you benefit from seminars by:

• Being aware of the value of seminars
• Focusing on links to learning
• Recognizing qualities you can use repeatedly
• Managing potential problems in seminars
• Preparing yourself adequately for seminars

An Asset to Complement other Learning Activities

Seminars are often optional in a degree programme and sometimes poorly attended because some students are convinced that lectures are the only way to get quality information, or that their time would be better spent in personal study. Actually all are of benefit, and seminars offer a unique contribution to learning that will complement lectures because they help you engage with – and better understand – course material by:

✓ clarifying terms, discussing issues and getting examples

✓ identifying problems or different perspectives that you had not thought of

✓ allowing you to ask questions and make comments

✓ helping you develop friendships and teamwork

✓ enabling you to refresh and consolidate your knowledge

✓ helping you sharpen motivation and redirect study efforts.

Don't underestimate them! The seminar holds an important place within the overall scheme of teaching, learning and assessment where a variety of methods are often used. In some programmes the seminars are directly linked to the assessment task. Whether or not they have such a place in your course, they will provide you with a unique opportunity to learn and develop.

A key question that you should bring to every seminar – 'How does this seminar connect with my other learning activities and my assessments?'

In a seminar you will hear a variety of contributions, and different perspectives and emphases. You will have the chance to interrupt and the experience of being interrupted! You will also learn that you can get things wrong and still survive! It is often the case that when one student admits that they did not know some important piece of information, other students quickly follow on to the same admission in the wake of this. If you can learn to ask questions and not feel stupid, then seminars will give you an asset for learning and a life-long learning.

Creating the Right Climate in Seminars

It has been said that we have been given only one mouth to talk, but two ears to listen. One potential problem with seminars is that some students may take a while to learn this lesson. In lectures your main role is to listen and take notes, but in seminars you need to strike the balance between listening and speaking. It's also important to disagree in an agreeable way, without attacking the other person. For example, you might question what someone else has said by saying 'That's a good point. What if we thought about it from this perspective...' rather than 'that was a really stupid thing to say', or 'I'm surprised that you don't know that by now.' The first approach encourages constructive debate and is a great skill to take through work and personal life!

Your lecturer may run the seminars, but may also ask students to take the lead. Here are some suggestions to help you with this task:

- Appoint someone to guide and control the discussion.
- Invite individuals to prepare in advance to make a contribution.
- Hand out agreed discussion questions prior to the seminar so that people are prepared.
- Stress at the beginning that everyone should contribute and respect the views of others (state clearly what this means).
- Encourage quieter students to participate and assure each person that their contribution is valued.

Links in Learning and Transferable Skills

An important principle in maximizing your learning is developing the capacity to make connections between themes, topics and across subjects. This also applies to the various learning activities such as lectures, seminars, fieldwork, case studies, computer searches and private study. Another factor to think about is, 'what skills can I develop, or improve from seminars that I can use across my study programme?' A couple of examples of key skills are the ability to communicate and the capacity to work within a team. These are skills that you will be able to use at various points in your course – and your career – but are not likely to learn in a lecture.

> *Think about what you personally can get out of seminars and what skills you could develop that will help you in the future.*

An Opportunity to Contribute

If you haven't been to seminars before, then it can be difficult to speak for the first time, but just say something – even if it is a question or to say you agree with something. It doesn't matter if your first contribution is only a sentence or two – the important thing is to make a start. One way to do this is to make brief notes as others contribute, and whilst doing this, a question or two might arise in your mind. Or it may be that you will be able to point out some connection between what others have said, or identify conflicting opinions that need to be resolved. If you have already begun making contributions, it is important that you keep the momentum going, and do not allow yourself to lapse back into shyness. It does get easier and your confidence will increase! Remember your opinions and ideas are as valid as anyone else's.

Strategies for Benefiting from your Seminar Experience

In order to benefit from discussions in seminars, the following will help:

- ✓ Do some preparatory reading
- ✓ Familiarize yourself with the main ideas to be addressed
- ✓ Make notes during the seminar
- ✓ Make some verbal contribution, even a question
- ✓ Remind yourself of the skills you can develop
- ✓ Trace learning links from the seminar to other subjects/topics on your programme
- ✓ Make brief bullet points on what you need to follow up
- ✓ Read over your notes as soon as possible after the seminar
- ✓ Continue discussion with fellow students after the seminar has ended

If required to give a presentation:

- ✓ Have a practice run with friends
- ✓ If using visuals, do not obstruct them
- ✓ Check out beforehand that all equipment works
- ✓ Space out points clearly on visuals (large and legible)
- ✓ Time talk by visuals (e.g. 5 slides in a 15 minute talk = 3 minutes per slide)

- ✓ Make sure your talk synchronizes with the slide on view at any given point
- ✓ Project your voice so that all in the room can hear
- ✓ Inflect your voice and do not stand motionless
- ✓ Spread eye contact around the audience
- ✓ Avoid twin extremes of fixed gaze at individuals and never looking at anyone
- ✓ Better to fall a little short of time allocation than run over it
- ✓ Be selective in what you choose to present
- ✓ Map out where you are going and summarize main points at the end

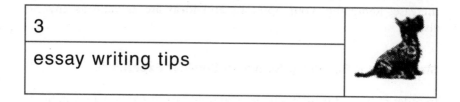

3

essay writing tips

This section will help you develop successful essay writing techniques and skills. There are a number of guidelines that will help you plan and write a well-structured essay. There are study skills books that deal with this issue in depth, but this section will help you to:

- Engage quickly with the main arguments
- Channel your ideas and interests constructively
- Note your main arguments in an outline
- Find and focus on your central topic questions
- Weave quotations into your essay

Getting into the Flow

In essay writing one of your first aims should be to engage with your subject. Tennis players like to go out onto the court and hit the ball back and forth just before the competitive match begins to get a sense of the bounce of the ball, the height of the net, the parameters of the court and so on. In the same way you can 'warm up' for your essay by playing with the ideas and thinking about what you want to say and the most effective way of saying it before you begin to write. This will allow you to think within the framework of your topic, and will be especially important if you are coming to the subject for the first time.

The Tributary Principle

A tributary is a stream that runs into a main river as it wends its way to the sea. Similarly in an essay you should ensure that every idea you introduce is moving toward the overall theme you are addressing. Your idea might of course be relevant to a subheading that is in turn relevant to a main heading. Every idea you introduce is to be a 'feeder' into the flowing theme. In addition to tributaries, there can also be 'distributaries', which are streams that flow away from the river. In an essay these would represent the ideas that run away from the main stream of thought and leave the reader trying to work out what their relevance may be. It is one thing to have grasped your subject thoroughly, but quite another to convince your reader that this is the case. Your aim should be to build up ideas sentence-by-sentence and paragraph-by-paragraph, until you have communicated your clear purpose to the reader.

> *It is important in essay writing that you do not only include material that is relevant, but that you also make the linking statements that show the connection to the reader. Use statements like 'having looked at the organization structure that would be most appropriate to the environmental demands, it is now important to address which design factors would work best'.*

Listing and linking the key concepts

All subjects will have central concepts that can sometimes be usefully labelled by a single word. Course textbooks may include a glossary of terms and these provide a direct route to efficient mastery of the topic. The central words or terms are the essential raw materials that you will need to build upon. Ensure that you learn the words and their definitions, and that you can go on to link the key words together so that you can explain the connections and relationships in an essay.

> *It is useful to list your key words under general headings if that is possible and logical. You may not always see the connections immediately but when you later come back to a problem that seemed intractable, you will often find that your thinking is much clearer.*

EXAMPLE   **Write an essay on 'Under what conditions might a functional organization structure be most appropriate?'**

Textbooks discuss this in a fairly straightforward way, so make sure you review the relevant material. Clarify your instructor's expectations. Is she/he looking for a straightforward analysis, a critical analysis, for further research...? Depending on these expectations:

1 Don't describe the structure and design factors – most essays and case study analyses are not based on recalling information (unless your instructor specifically asks you to do so), but on making links between the ideas and theories. So don't say, 'A functional organization is highly differentiated. There are two types of differentiation, the first is vertical differentiation which means...'

2 Do use the terminology (organic, differentiation, formalization, etc.) – this indicates you've read your textbook!

3 *Apply* the design factors and principles to the question – this shows you understand the material. In other words, say, 'One of the factors influencing the suitability of a functional structure is whether the goal of the organization is to produce a large quantity of the product, or produce a consistent and high quality service to customers. For example, Federal Express ... In this situation a functional structure is most appropriate because formal rules and procedures (a key design factor in a functional structure) ensure that all employees know what work needs to be done to achieve the goal of timely delivery... Similarly the standardization of work practices leads to a cost efficient service which allows FedEx to be competitive... Another factor is the type of environment the organization operates within (Burns and Stalker, 1966)...'

Make a list of the key points, or draw a mind map before you begin writing so that you know what needs to be included and in what order.

An Adversarial System

In higher education students are required to make the transition from descriptive to critical writing. If you can, think of the critical approach as a law case that is being conducted where there is both a prosecution and a defence. Your concern should be for objectivity, transparency and fairness. No matter how passionately you may feel about a given cause you must not allow information to be filtered out because of your personal prejudice. An essay should not become a crusade for a cause in which the contrary arguments are not addressed in an evenhanded manner. This means that you should show awareness that opposite views are held and you should at least represent these as accurately as possible.

> *Your role as the writer is like that of the judge in that you must ensure that all the evidence is heard, and that the conclusion (outcome) is based on the evidence.*

Stirring up Passions

The above points do not of course mean that you are not entitled to a personal opinion or to feel passionately about your subject. On the contrary such feelings may well be a marked advantage if you can bring them under control and channel them into balanced, effective writing (see example below). Remember, some students may be struggling with the opposite problem – writing about a topic they feel quite indifferent about. As you engage with your topic and toss the ideas around in your mind, you will hopefully find that your interest is stimulated, if only at an intellectual level initially. How strongly you feel about a topic, or how much you are interested in it, may depend on whether you choose the topic yourself or whether it has been given to you as an obligatory assignment. If the latter, you still need to research the issue and present a persuasive argument – your grade will depend upon it!

> *It is important that in a large project (such as a dissertation) you choose a topic for which you can maintain your motivation, momentum and enthusiasm.*

For example, the topic of technology might seem boring, especially if like me you are technologically challenged! In this case one of the best things you can do if you have to write about it is bring technology to life – go on company tours and factory visits to observe technology in operation. I've dragged my daughter around beer-making, glass-making, chocolate-making, paper-making tours, as well as visiting ball-bearing and felt-making companies! As you go round the tour, think about the type of technology, it's complexity, and how people interact with the technology. For example, beer-making is a continuous process technology (Woodward), long-linked (Thompson), with low task variety and high analysability (Perrow), with little human interaction as employees monitor an automated process... and you get free samples of the product at the end of the tour!

Structuring an Outline

Structure and order facilitate good communication – so put your ideas and inspirations into a structure that will allow the marker to recognize the true quality of your work. For example, you might plan for an Introduction, Conclusion, three main headings and each of these with several subheadings (see example below). Moreover, you may decide not to include your headings in your final presentation – i.e. just use them initially to structure and balance your arguments. Once you have drafted this outline you can then easily sketch an Introduction, and you will have been well prepared for the Conclusion when you arrive at that point.

> *A good structure will help you to balance the weight of each of your arguments against each other, and arrange your points in the order that will facilitate the fluent progression of your argument.*

EXAMPLE   Can organization culture be managed? If so, how – if not, why not?

You will be most likely to get this question if your OT textbook takes a critical perspective because it requires you to think about both sides of the argument – that culture can be managed – and that there are those who say it cannot be.

1 Culture can be managed:

- A number of theorists talk about 'excellent' cultures (Peters and Waterman), or the need for more humanistic cultures (Ouchi) and assume that managers can take the characteristics of these cultures and implement them in their organizations.
- Culture may need to be managed as environmental demands change or if an unproductive culture exists. Can do this through mimetic isomorphism.
- By creating appropriate mission, vision and values statements (give examples).

- Through ceremonies and rituals (example).
- Through symbols and artifacts.
- The key is not just creating these but obtaining commitment from employees.
- Culture can be over-managed.

2 Culture cannot be managed:

- Postmodern organization theorists see culture as fragmented and valueless.
- Culture is always shifting and out of any person's control (e.g., Boje's work).
- Managing culture privileges particular ideologies and marginalizes groups, so should be overturned.
- Unofficial cultures exist that have just as much influence as official ones (Watson).

Finding Major Questions

When you are constructing a draft outline for an essay or project, you should ask what is the major question or questions your lecturer wishes you to address. Then make a list of all the issues that spring to mind that you need to tackle. Or you might be asked to identify the question yourself. The ability to design a good question is an art form that should be cultivated, and such questions will allow you to impress your assessor with the quality of your thinking.

If you construct your ideas around key questions, this will help you focus your mind and engage effectively with your subject. Your role will be like that of a detective – exploring the evidence and investigating the findings.

To illustrate the point, consider the example presented below. If you are asked to write an essay about the effectiveness of the structure and design factors in your organization, you might pose the following questions:

EXAMPLE   The effectiveness of my organization's structure and design.

- What does 'effectiveness' mean?
- What is the organization's structure?
- What are the organization's design factors?

- What are the environmental factors, complexity, etc?
- What life cycle stage is my organization at?
- Do these 'fit'?

Rest your Case

Aim to give the clear impression that your arguments are not based entirely on hunches, bias, feelings or intuition. In exams and essay questions it is usually assumed (even if not directly specified) that you will appeal to evidence to support your claims. Therefore, when you write your essay you should ensure you include citations, evidence and examples. By the time the assessor reaches the end of your work, he or she should be convinced that your conclusions are evidence-based. Avoid making claims for which you have provided no authoritative source.

> *Give the clear impression that your assertions are derived from recognized and up-to-date sources. It also looks impressive if you spread your citations across your essay rather than compressing them into a paragraph or two at the beginning and end.*

Some examples of how you might introduce your evidence and sources are provided below:

According to O'Neil (1999) ...
Wilson (2003) has concluded that ...
Taylor (2004) found that ...
It has been claimed by McKibben (2002) that ...
Appleby (2001) asserted that ...
A review of the evidence by Lawlor (2004) suggests that ...
Findings from a meta-analysis presented by Rea (2003) would indicate that ...

It is sensible to vary the expression used so that you are not monotonous and repetitive, and it also aids variety to introduce researchers' names at various places in the sentence (not always at the beginning). It is advisable to choose the expression that is most appropriate – for example, you can make a stronger statement about reviews that have identified recurrent and predominant trends in findings as opposed to one study that appears to run contrary to all the rest. Do remember to fully reference any evidence included in tables, graphs, etc.

> *Credit is given for the use of caution and discretion when this is clearly needed.*

Careful Use of Quotations

Although it is desirable to present a good range of cited sources, it is not judicious to present these as a 'patchwork quilt' – i.e. you just paste together what others have said with little thought for interpretative comment or coherent structure. It is a good general point to avoid very lengthy quotes – short ones can be more effective. Aim at blending the quotations as naturally as possible into the flow of your sentences. Also it is good to vary your practices – sometimes use short, direct, brief quotes (cite page number as well as author and year), and at times you can summarize the gist of a quote in your own words. In this case you should cite the author's name and year of publication but leave out quotation marks and page number.

> *Use your quotes and evidence in a manner that demonstrates that you have thought the issues through, and have integrated them in a manner that shows you have been focused and selective in the use of your sources.*

Referencing demonstrates your knowledge of the literature and your understanding of how the work of authors contributes to your argument. How to reference varies from one discipline to the next, but some general points that will go a long way in contributing to good practice are:

- If a reference is cited in the text, it must be listed in the 'References' or 'Bibliography' at the end (and vice-versa).
- Names and dates in text should correspond exactly with the list in the References or Bibliography.
- The list of References and Bibliography should be in alphabetical order by the surname (not the initials) of the author or first author.
- Any reference you make in the text should be traceable by the reader (they should clearly be able to identify and trace the source).

A Clearly Defined Introduction

Remember the golden rule: 'Tell them what you are going to say, Tell them, and Tell them what you said'. In an introduction to an essay you have the opportunity to define the problem or issue that is being addressed, to set it within context and outline briefly how you will address it. Resist the temptation to elaborate on any issue at the introductory stage. For example, think of a music composer who throws out hints and suggestions of the motifs that the orchestra will later develop. What he or she does in the introduction is to provide little tasters of what will follow in order to whet the audience's appetite.

If you leave the introduction and definition of your problem until the end of your writing, you will be better placed to map out the directions that will be taken.

Conclusion – Adding the Finishing Touches

In the conclusion you should aim to tie your essay together in a clear and coherent manner. It is your last chance to leave an overall impression in your reader's mind. Therefore, you will at this stage want to outline what you did and to justify your efforts. Identify your strongest evidence points, a brief summary of the arguments for and against, or your key argument. The conclusion to an exam question often has to be written hurriedly under the pressure of time, but with an essay (course work) you have time to reflect on, refine and adjust the content to your satisfaction. It should be your goal to make the conclusion a smooth finish that does justice to the range of content in summary and succinct form. Do not under-estimate the value of an effective conclusion. 'Sign off' your essay in a manner that brings closure to the treatment of your subject.

The conclusion is your chance to demonstrate where the findings have brought us to date, to highlight the issues that remain unresolved and to point to where future research should take us.

Top-down and Bottom-up Clarity

Your computer gives you the opportunity to refine each sentence and paragraph of your essay. Each sentence is like a tributary that leads into the stream of the paragraph that in turn leads into the mainstream of the essay. From a 'top-down' perspective (i.e. starting at the top with your major outline points), clarity is facilitated by the structure you draft in your outline. You can ensure that the subheadings are appropriately placed under the most relevant main heading, and that both sub and main headings are arranged in logical sequence. From a 'bottom-up' perspective (i.e. building up the details that 'flesh out' your main points), you should check that each sentence is a 'feeder' for the predominant concept in a given paragraph. When all this is done you can check that the transition from one point to the next is smooth rather than abrupt.

Checklist – summary for essay writing

- ✓ Before you start – have a 'warm up' by tossing the issues around in your head
- ✓ List the major concepts and link them in fluent form
- ✓ Design a structure (outline) that will facilitate balance, progression, fluency and clarity
- ✓ Pose questions and address these in critical fashion
- ✓ Demonstrate that your arguments rest on evidence and spread cited sources across your essay
- ✓ Provide an Introduction that sets the scene and a Conclusion that rounds off the arguments

In the above checklist you could include features such as originality, clarity in sentence and paragraph structure, applied aspects, addressing a subject you feel passionately about and the ability to avoid going off on a tangent.

4	
revision hints and tips	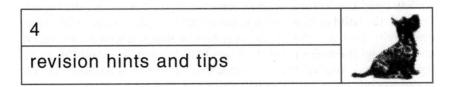

This section will show you how to:

- Map out your accumulated material for revision
- Choose summary tags to guide your revision

- Keep well-organized folders for revision
- Make use of effective memory techniques
- Revise combining bullet points and in-depth reading
- Profit from the benefits of revising with others
- Attend to the practical exam details that will help keep panic at bay
- Use strategies that keep you task-focused during the exam
- Select and apply relevant points from your prepared outlines

The Return Journey

This Companion presents a travel guide to the key concepts and issues in OT. If you read the relevant chapters before your class, then it offers signposts to look for on the journey. In the same sense, on the return journey you will usually pass by all the same places and should recollect the various landmarks on your return. Similarly, revision is a means to 'revisit' what you have encountered before. Familiarity with your material can help reduce anxiety, inspire confidence and fuel motivation for further learning and good performance.

If you are to capitalize on your revision period, then you must have your materials arranged and at hand for the time when you are ready to make your 'return journey' through your notes.

Start at the Beginning

A strategy for revision should be on your mind from your first lecture at the beginning of your academic semester. It can save you a lot of time and anxiety later! Use lecture, tutorial, seminar, group discussion, etc. by getting into the habit of making a few guidelines for revision after each learning activity. Keep a folder, or file, or notebook that is reserved for revision and write out the major points that you have learned. By establishing this regular practice you will find that what you have learned becomes consolidated in your mind, and you will also be in a better position to transfer your material both within and across subjects.

If you do this regularly, and do not make the task too tedious, you will be amazed at how much useful summary material you have accumulated when revision time comes.

When studying OT, it is particularly helpful to get examples of organizational structure, culture, etc. from case studies, newspapers, TV and the Internet. You will find some useful resources in the Additional Reading sections in Part 2 and the References.

Compile Summary Notes

It is useful and convenient to have a notebook or cards with outline summaries that provide you with an overview of your subject at a glance. You could also use treasury tags to hold different batches of cards together whilst still allowing for inserts and re-sorting. Such practical resources can easily be slipped into your pocket or bag and produced when you are on the bus or train or whilst sitting in a traffic jam. They would also be useful if you are standing in a queue or waiting for someone who is not in a rush! A glance over your notes will consolidate your learning and will also activate your mind to think further about your subject. Therefore it would also be useful to make note of the questions that you would like to think about in greater depth. Your primary task is to get into the habit of constructing outline notes that will be useful for revision, and a worked example is provided below.

There is a part of the mind that will continue to work on problems when you have moved on to focus on other issues. Therefore, if you feed on useful, targeted information, your mind will continue to work on 'automatic pilot' after you have 'switched off'.

EXAMPLE   Organization structure and design.

Your outline revision structure might be as follows:

1 *Difference between organization structure and design*

- Structure is the basic framework of the organization
- Design is all the elements that make up the structure

2 *Types of structures*

- Functional (bureaucracy?)
- Divisional: product/service, geographic, market/customer
- Matrix
- Hybrid, strategic alliances and joint ventures, multinational and global, network and virtual

3 *Design factors*

- Differentiation
- Integration
- Centralization/decentralization
- Standardization/mutual adjustment
- Formalization
- Mechanistic/organic

You might have other related cards or pages in your notebook on: why OT is important, the advantages and disadvantages of each structure, and so on.

Keep Organized Records

People who have a fulfilled career have usually developed the twin skills of time and task management. It is worth pausing to remember that you can use your academic training to prepare for your future career in this respect. Therefore, ensure that you do not fall short of your potential because these qualities have not been cultivated. One important tactic is to keep a folder for each subject and divide this topic-by-topic. You can keep your topics in the same order in which they are presented in your course lecture in a ring binder or folder, and use subject dividers to keep them apart. Make a numbered list of the contents at the beginning of the folder, and list each topic clearly as it marks a new section in your folder. Another important practice is to place all your notes on a given topic within the appropriate section and don't put off this simple task, do it straightaway. Notes may come from lectures, seminars, tutorials, Internet searches, personal notes, etc. It is also essential that when you remove these for consultation that you return them to their 'home' immediately after use.

> Academic success has as much to do with good organization and planning, as it has to do with ability. The value of the quality material you have accumulated on your academic programme may be diminished because you have not organized it into an easily retrievable form.

EXAMPLE   Fun example of an organized record – a history of romantic relationships

- Physical features my girlfriends/boyfriends have shared or differed
- Common and diverse personality characteristics

- Shared and contrasting interests
- Frequency of dates with each
- Places frequented together
- Contact with both circles of friends
- Use of humour in our communication
- Frequency and resolution of conflicts
- Mutual generosity
- Courtesy and consideration
- Punctuality
- Dress and appearance

Let's imagine that you had three girlfriends/boyfriends over the last few years. Each of the three names could be included under all of the above subjects. You could then compare them with each other – looking at what they had in common and how they differed. Moreover, you could think of the ones you liked best and least, and then look through your dossier to establish why this might have been. You could also judge who had most and least in common with you and whether you are more attracted to those who differed most from you. The questions open to you can go on and on. The real point here is that you will have gathered a wide variety of material that is organized in such a way that will allow you to use a range of evidence to come up with some satisfactory and authoritative conclusions – if that is possible in matters so directly related to the heart!

Use Past Papers

Revision will be very limited if it is confined to memory work. You should by all means read over your revision cards or notebook and keep the picture of the major facts in front of your mind's eye. It is also, however, essential that you become familiar with previous exam papers so that you will have some idea of how the questions are likely to be framed. Therefore, build up a good range of past exam papers (especially recent ones) and add these to your folder.

> If you think over previous exam questions, this will help you not only recall what you have deposited in your memory, but also to develop your understanding of the issues. The questions from past exam papers, and further questions that you have developed yourself, will allow you to 'chew the cud'.

Look at what the questions ask you to do: discuss, analyse, evaluate... 'Discuss' means looking at all points of view and assessing implications.

'Analyse' means looking at causes and implications. 'Evaluate' means making an informed judgement by working through all the issues from different standpoints. So ensure that part of your revision includes critical thinking as well as memory work.

> You cannot think adequately without the raw materials provided by your memory deposits.

Employ Effective Mnemonics (memory aids)

The Greek word from which 'mnemonics' is derived, refers to a tomb – a structure that is built in memory of a loved one, friend or respected person. 'Mnemonics' can be simply defined as aids to memory – devices that will help you recall information that might otherwise be difficult to retrieve from memory. For example, if you find an old toy in the attic of your house, it may suddenly trigger a flood of childhood memories associated with it. Mnemonics can therefore be thought of as keys that open memory's storehouse.

> 1   If you can arrange your subject matter in a logical sequence this will ensure that your series of facts will also connect with each other and one will trigger the other in recall.
> 2   You can use memory devices either at the stage of initial learning or when you later return to consolidate.

Visualization is one technique that can be used to aid memory. For example, the location method is where a familiar journey is visualized and you can 'place' the facts that you wish to remember at various landmarks along the journey – e.g., a bus stop, a car park, a shop, a store, a bend, a police station, a traffic light, etc. This has the advantage of making an association of the information you have to learn with other material that is already firmly embedded and structured in your memory. Therefore, once the relevant memory is activated, a dynamic 'domino effect' will be triggered. However, there is no reason why you cannot use a whole toolkit of mnemonics. Some examples and illustrations of these are presented below.

- *Visualization* – Turn information into pictures, e.g. when thinking about organization culture, have a particular organization in mind, visualize a vision statement on its webpage, or walking through the building looking at symbols and artefacts, the décor, how people interact, and so on.
- *Alliteration's artful aid* – Find a series of words that all begin with the same letter. See the example below related to the experiments of Ebbinghaus.
- *Peg system* – 'Hang' information on to a term so that when you hear the term you will remember the ideas connected with it (an umbrella term). In the example on organization structure and design think about the six pegs of which differentiation and integration are the first two.
- *Hierarchical system* – This is a development of the previous point with higher order, middle order and lower order terms. For example, you could think of the continents of the world (higher order), and then group these into the countries under them (middle order). Under countries you could have cities, rivers and mountains (lower order).
- *Acronyms* – Take the first letter of all the key words and make a word from these. An example from strategy is SWOT – Strengths, Weaknesses, Opportunities and Threats.
- *Mind maps* – These have become very popular – they allow you to develop ideas using lines that stretch out from the central idea, and to develop the subsidiary ideas in the same way. It is a little like the pegging and hierarchical methods combined and turned sideways! The method has the advantage of giving you the complete picture at a glance, although they can become a complex work of art!
- *Rhymes and chimes* – Words that rhyme and words that end with a similar sound (e.g. commemoration, celebration, anticipation). These provide another dimension to memory work by including sound. Memory can be enhanced when information is processed in various modalities – e.g. hearing, seeing, speaking, visualizing.

A Confidence Booster

At the end of the nineteenth century, Ebbinghaus and his assistant memorized lists of nonsense words (words that could not be remembered by being attached to meaning), and then endeavoured to recall these. They discovered:

- Some words could be recalled freely from memory while others appeared to be forgotten.
- Words that could not be recalled were later recognized as belonging to the lists (i.e. were not new additions).
- When the lists were jumbled into a different sequence, the experimenters were able to re-jumble them into the original sequence.

- When the words that were 'forgotten' were learned again, the learning process was much easier the second time (i.e. there was evidence of re-learning savings).

The four points of this experiment can be remembered by alliteration: Recall, Recognition, Reconstruction and Re-learning savings. This experiment has been described as a confidence booster because it demonstrates that memory is more powerful than is often imagined, especially when we consider that Ebbinghaus and his assistant did not have the advantage of processing the meaning of the words.

Alternate between Reading and Making Artlines

It is not sufficient to present outline points in response to an exam question (although it is better to do this than do nothing if you have run out of time in your exam). Your aim should be to put 'meat on the bones' by adding substance, evidence and arguments to your basic points. You should work at finding the balance between the two methods – outline revision cards might be best reserved for short bus journeys, whereas extended reading might be better employed for longer revision slots at home or in the library. Your ultimate goal should be to bring together an effective, working approach that will enable you to face your exam questions comprehensively and confidently.

> *In revision it is useful to alternate between scanning over your outline points, and reading through your notes, articles, chapters etc. in an in-depth manner. Also, the use of different times, places and methods will provide you with the variety that might prevent monotony and facilitate freshness.*

WORKED EXAMPLE   A course on Organization Theory.

Your major outline topics might be:

- What is OT and why is it important?
- Organization structure and design
- Technology and its impact on structure and design
- Organization culture and its relationship to structure, design, strategy, ethics, etc.
- The relationship between environment, strategy and structure
- Power, conflict and control
- Organizational innovation, change and learning
- How do all the pieces fit?

This outline would be your overall, bird's eye view of the course. You could then choose one of the topics and have all your key terms under that. Fill in the gaps by reading about the key issues and debates in each topic. Then think about how the topics relate to each other.

If you alternate between memory work and reading, you will soon be able to think through the processes by just looking at your outlines.

Revising with Others

If you can find a few other students to revise with, this will provide another fresh approach to the last stages of your learning. First ensure that others carry their work load and are not merely using the hard work of others as a short cut to success. Of course you should think of group sessions as one of the strings on your violin, but not the only string. This collective approach would allow you to assess your strengths and weaknesses (showing you where you are off track), and to benefit from the resources and insights of others. Before you meet up you can each design some questions for the whole group to address. The group could also go through past exam papers and discuss the points that might provide an effective response to each question. It should not be the aim of the group to provide standard and identical answers for each group member to mimic. Group work is currently deemed to be advantageous by educationalists, as well as a desirable employability quality.

Each individual should aim to use their own style and content whilst drawing on and benefiting from the group's resources.

Checklist – good study habits for revision time

✓ Set a date for the 'official' beginning of revision and prepare for 'revision mode'
✓ Do not force cramming by leaving revision too late
✓ Take breaks from revision to avoid saturation
✓ Indulge in relaxing activities to give your mind a break from pressure
✓ Minimize or eliminate use of alcohol during the revision season

✓ Get into a good rhythm of sleep to allow renewal of your mind
✓ Avoid excessive caffeine especially at night so that sleep is not disrupted
✓ Try to adhere to regular eating patterns
✓ Try to have a brisk walk in fresh air each day (e.g. in the park)
✓ Avoid excessive dependence on junk food and snacks

What would you add to this list? Using past exam papers, setting problem solving tasks, drawing mind maps, explaining concepts to student friends in joint revision sessions, devising your own mock exam questions...

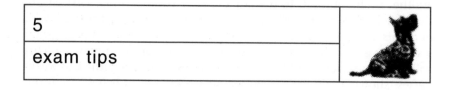

5	
exam tips	

This section is designed to help you succeed in your exams. It will provide you with tips on how to:

• Develop strategies for controlling your nervous energy
• Tackle worked examples of time and task management in exams
• Attend to the practical details associated with the exam
• Stay focused on the exam questions
• Link revision outlines to strategy for addressing exam questions

Handling Your Nerves

Exam nerves are common because your performance is being evaluated, the consequences are likely to be serious, and you are working under the pressure of a time restriction. However, adrenalin can also help us focus, be attentive and creative! The key is to focus on the positive and try to keep your nerves under control. In the run up to your exams you can practise some simple relaxation techniques that will help you bring stress under control.

> Interpret your nervous reactions positively – if you pay too much attention to the negative they can interfere with your exam preparation or performance. Take a deep breath!

Practices that may help reduce or buffer the effects of exam stress:

- Listening to music
- Going for a brisk walk
- Simple breathing exercises
- Going to yoga
- Watching a movie
- Enjoying some laughter
- Doing some exercise
- Relaxing in a bath (with music if preferred)

Find the one (or combination) that works best for you – perhaps to be discovered by trial and error. Some of the above techniques can be practised on the morning of the exam, and even the memory of them can be used just before the exam. For example, you could run over a relaxing tune in your head, and have this echo inside you as you enter the exam room. The idea behind all this is, first, stress levels must come down, and second, relaxing thoughts will serve to displace stressful reactions. It has been said that stress is the body's call to take action, but anxiety is a maladaptive response to that call.

> It is important you are convinced that your stress levels can come under control, and that you can have a say in this. Do not give anxiety a vacuum to work in.

Exam Time Management

The all-important matter as you approach an exam is to develop the belief that you can take control over the situation. As you work through the list of issues that you need to address, you will be able to tick them off one by one. One of the issues you will need to be clear about before the exam is the length of time you should allocate to each question. Sometimes this can be quite simple (although it is always necessary to read the rubric carefully) – e.g. if two questions are to be answered in a two hour exam, you should allow one hour for each question. If it is a two-hour exam with one essay question and five shorter answers, you could allow one hour for the essay and 12 minutes each for the shorter questions. However, you always need to check out the weighting for the marks on each question, and you will also need to deduct whatever time it takes you to read over the paper and to choose your questions. See if you can work out a time management strategy in each of the following scenarios. More importantly, give yourself some practice on the papers you are likely to face.

> *Remember to check if the structure of your exam paper is the same as in previous years, and do not forget that excessive time on your 'strongest' question may not compensate for very poor answers to other questions. Also ensure that you read the rubric carefully in the exam.*

EXERCISE

Examples and suggested answers for working out the division of exam labour by time:

1. A 3-hour exam with 4 compulsory questions (equally weighted in marks).

    This allows 45 minutes for each question (4 questions x 45 minutes = 3 hours). However, if you allow 40 minutes for each question this will give you 20 minutes (4 questions x 5 minutes) to read over the paper and plan your outlines.

2. A 3-hour exam with 2 essays and 10 short questions (each of the three sections carry one third of the marks).

    In this example you can spend 1 hour on each of the two major questions, and 1 hour on the 10 short questions. For the two major questions you could allow 10 minutes for reading and planning on each, and 50 minutes for writing. In the 10 short questions, you could allow 6 minutes in total for each (10 questions x 6 minutes = 60 minutes). However, if you allow approximately 1 minute reading and planning time, this will allow 5 minutes writing time for each question.

3. A 2-hour exam with 2 essay questions and 100 multiple-choice questions (half marks are on the two essays and half marks on the multiple choice section).

    In this case you have to divide 120 minutes by 3 questions – this allows 40 minutes for each. You could, for example, allow 5 minutes reading/planning time for each essay and 35 minutes for writing (or 10 minutes reading/planning and 30 minutes writing). After you have completed the two major questions you are left with 40 minutes to tackle the 100 multiple-choice questions.

Have the calculations done before the exam. Ensure that the structure of the exam has not changed since the last one. Also deduct the time taken to read over the paper in allocating time to each question. This will give you greater control and confidence, even though you might have to change your plan slightly as you go.

Task Management with Examples

After you have decided on the questions, you then need to plan your answers. Some students prefer to plan all outlines and draft work at the beginning, whilst others prefer to plan and address one answer before proceeding to address the next question. Decide on your strategy before you enter the exam room and stick to your plan. When you have done your draft outline as rough work, you should allocate appropriate timing for each section. This will prevent you from excessive treatment of some aspects whilst falling short on other parts. Such careful planning will help you achieve balance, fluency and symmetry.

Keep awareness of time limitations and this will help you to write succinctly, keep focused on the task and prevent you dressing up your responses with unnecessary padding.

Some students put as much effort into their rough work as they do into their exam essay. Don't spend too much time on your plan at the expense of writing your answer.

EXERCISE

Work out the time allocation for the following outline allowing for 1 hour on the question. Deduct 10 minutes taken at the beginning for choice and planning.

'Discuss whether it is justifiable to ban cigarette smoking in pubs and restaurants.'

1. Arguments for a ban

    a. Health risks by sustained exposure to passive smoking
    b. Employees (such as students) suffer unfairly
    c. Children with parents may also be victims

2. Arguments against a ban

   a. Risks may be exaggerated

   b. Dangerous chemicals and pollutants in environment ignored by governments

   c. Non-smokers can choose whether to frequent smoking venues

3. Qualifying suggestions

   a. Better use of ventilation and extractor fans

   b. Designated non-smoking areas

   c. Pubs and restaurants should be addressed separately in relation to a ban

Attend to Practical Details

This short section is designed to remind you of the practical details that should be attended to in preparation for an exam. There are always students who turn up late, or to the wrong venue, or for the wrong exam, or do not turn up at all! Check and re-check that you have all the details of each exam correctly noted. What you don't need is to arrive late and then have to tame your panic reactions. The exam season is the time when you should aim to be at your best. I also have students who arrive at the exam without anything to write with!

> *Turn up to the right venue in good time so that you can calm your mind and bring your stress under control.*

Make note of the following details and check that you have taken control of each one.

Checklist – practical exam details

✓ Check that you have the correct venue

✓ Make sure you know how to locate the venue before the exam day

✓ Ensure that the exam time you have noted is accurate

✓ Allow sufficient time for your journey and consider the possibility of delays

✓ Bring an adequate supply of paper and include back up

✓ Bring a watch for your time and task management

✓ You may need some liquid such as a small bottle of still water

✓ You may also need to bring some tissues

✓ Observe whatever exam regulations your university/college has set in place

✓ Fill in required personal details before the exam begins

Control Wandering Thoughts

In a simple study conducted in the 1960s, Ganzer found that students who frequently lifted their heads and looked away from their scripts during exams tended to perform poorly. This makes sense because it implies that the students were taking too much time out when they should have been on task. One way to fail your exam is to get up and walk out of the test room, but another way is to 'leave' the test room mentally by being preoccupied with distracting thoughts. The distracting thoughts may be either related to the exam itself or totally irrelevant to it. The net effect of both these forms of intrusion is to distract you from the task at hand and debilitate your test performance. Read over the two lists of distracting thoughts presented below.

Typical test-relevant thoughts (evaluative)

- I wish I had prepared better
- What will the examiner think
- Others are doing better than me
- What I am writing is nonsense
- Can't remember important details

Characteristic test-irrelevant thoughts (non-evaluative)

- Looking forward to this weekend
- Which video should I watch tonight?
- His remark really annoyed me yesterday
- Wonder how the game will go on Saturday
- I wonder if he/she really likes me?

Research has consistently shown that distracting, intrusive thoughts during an exam are more detrimental to performance than stressful symptoms such as sweaty palms, dry mouth, tension, trembling etc. Moreover, it does not matter whether the distracting thoughts are negative evaluations related to the exam or are totally irrelevant to the exam. The latter may be a form of escape from the stressful situation.

Practical suggestions for controlling wandering thoughts

- Be aware that this problem is detrimental to performance
- Do not look around to find distractions
- If distracted, breathe deeply and write 'keep focused on task'
- If distracted again, look back at above and continue to do this
- Start to draft rough work as soon as you can
- If you struggle with initial focus then re-read or elaborate on your rough work
- If you have commenced your essay, re-read your last paragraph (or two)
- Do not throw fuel on your distracting thoughts – starve them by re-engaging with the task at hand

Links to Revision

If you have followed the guidelines given for revision, you will be well equipped with outline plans when you enter the exam room. You may have chosen to use headings and subheadings, mind maps, hierarchical approaches or just a series of simple mnemonics. Whatever method you choose to use, you should be furnished with a series of memory triggers that will open the treasure house door for you once you begin to write.

Although you may have clear templates with a definite structure or framework for organizing your material, you will need to be flexible about how this should be applied to your exam questions.

For example, imagine that films are one of the topics that you will be examined on. You decide to memorize lists of films that you are familiar with under categorical headings in the following manner.

Romantic comedy	*War/History/Fantasy*	*Space/Invasion*
Notting Hill	Braveheart	Star Wars
Pretty Woman	Gladiator	Independence Day
Along came Polly	First Knight	Alien
Four Weddings and a Funeral	Troy	Men in Black

Adventure/Fantasy	*Horror/Supernatural*
Harry Potter	Poltergeist
Lord of the Rings	The Omen
Alice in Wonderland	Sixth Sense
Labyrinth	What Lies Beneath

The basic mental template might be these and a few other categories. You know that you will not need every last detail, although you may need to select a few from each category. For example you might be asked to:

(a) Compare and contrast features of comedy and horror.
(b) Comment on films that have realistic moral lessons in them.
(c) Evaluate films that might be construed as a propaganda exercise.
(d) Identify films where the characters are more important than the plot and vice-versa.

Some questions will put a restriction on the range of categories you can use (a), while others will allow you to dip into any category (b, c and d). A question about fantasy would allow you scope across various categories.

> *Restrict your material to what is relevant to the question, but bear in mind that this may allow you some scope.*

Art of 'Name Dropping'

In most topics at university you will be required to cite studies as evidence for your arguments and to link these to the names of researchers, scholars or theorists. This Course Companion identifies many of the classical and contemporary authors you need to know, and there will be many others in your textbook. Use your lecturer as a guide as she/he will also have identified key authors in class. It will help if you can use the correct dates or at least the decades, and it is good to demonstrate that you have used contemporary sources, and have done some independent work. A marker will have dozens if not hundreds of scripts to work through and they will know if you are just repeating the same phrases from the same sources as everyone else. There is inevitably a certain amount of this that must go on, but there is room for you to add fresh and original touches that demonstrate independence and imagination.

> *Give the clear impression that you have done more than the bare minimum and that you have enthusiasm for the subject. Also, spread the use of researchers' names across your exam essay rather than compressing them into, for example, the first and last paragraphs.*

Flight, Fight or Freeze

The autonomic nervous system (ANS) is activated when danger or apparent danger is imminent. Of course the threat does not have to be physical, as in the case of an exam, a job interview, a driving test or a TV appearance. Indeed the ANS can be activated even at the anticipation of a future threat. However, the reaction is more likely to be stronger as you enter into the crucial time of testing or challenge. Symptoms may include deep breathing, trembling, headaches, nausea, tension, dry mouth and palpitations. How should we react to these once they have been triggered? Do you run away from a barking dog and run the risk of being chased and bitten? A second possible response is to freeze on the spot – this might arrest the animal on its tracks, but is no use in an exam situation. In contrast, to fight might not be the best strategy against the dog, but will be more productive in an exam. That is, you are going into the exam room to 'tackle' the questions, and not to run away from the challenge before you.

The final illustration below uses the analogy of archery to demonstrate how you might take control in an exam.

- Enter the exam room with a quiver full of arrows – all the theories and key ideas you will need to use.
- Eye up the target board you are to shoot at – choose the exam questions carefully.
- Stand in good position for balance and vision – manage your time.
- Prepare your bow and arrow and take aim at the target – keep focused on the task at hand and don't get sidetracked.
- Pull the string of the bow back to get maximum thrust on the arrow – match your key points to the appropriate question.
- Aim to hit the board where the best marks are (bull's eye or close) – do not be content with the minimum standard such as a mere pass.
- Pull out arrows and shoot one after another to gain maximum hits and advantage – do not be content with preparing one or two strong points.
- Make sure your arrows are sharp and the supporting bow and string are firm – choose relevant points and support with theories, evidence and examples.
- Avoid wasted effort by loose and careless shots – do not dress up your essay with unnecessary padding.

EXERCISE

Write your own checklist on the range of combined skills and personal qualities that you will need to be at your best in an exam.

✓ ....
✓ ....
✓ ....
✓ ....
✓ ....

With reference to the above exercise – skills might include such things as critical thinking, time and task management, focus on issues, and quick identification of problems to address. Personal qualities might include factors such as confidence, endurance, resilience and stress control.

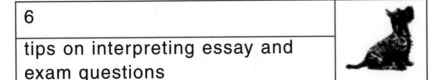

6
tips on interpreting essay and exam questions

Interpreting exam questions is not always easy. This section provides you with tips on how to:

- Focus on the issues that are relevant and central
- Read questions carefully and take account of all the words
- Produce a balanced critique in your outline structures
- Screen for the key words that will shape your response
- Focus on different shades of meaning between 'critique', 'evaluate', 'discuss' and 'compare and contrast'

What Do You See?

The suggested explanation for visual illusions is the inappropriate use of cues – i.e. we try to interpret three-dimensional figures in the real world with the limitations of a two-dimensional screen (the retina in the eye). We use cues such as shade, texture, size, background etc. to interpret

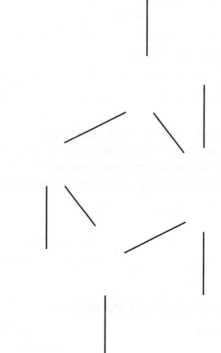

Figure 8   Visual illusion

distance, motion, shape etc., and we sometimes use these inappropri-
ately. Another visual practice we engage in is to 'fill in the blanks' or join
up the lines (as in the case of the nine lines above which we might
assume to be a chair). Our tendency is to impose the nearest similar and
familiar template on that which we think we see. The same occurs in the
social world – when we are introduced to someone of a different race we
may (wrongly) assume certain things about them. The same can also
.apply to the way you read exam or essay questions. In these cases you
are required to 'fill in the blanks' but what you fill in may be the wrong
interpretation of the question. This is especially likely if you have
primed yourself to expect certain questions to appear in an exam, but it
can also happen in course work essays. Although examiners do not
deliberately design questions to trick you or trip you up, they cannot
always prevent you from seeing things that were not designed to be
there. When one student was asked what the four seasons are, the

response given was, 'salt, pepper, mustard and vinegar'. This was not quite what the examiner had in mind!

Go into the exam room, or address the course work essay well prepared, but be flexible enough to structure your learned material around the slant of the question.

A Politician's Answer

Politicians are renowned for refusing to answer questions directly or for evading them through raising other questions. A humorous example is that when a politician was asked, 'Is it true that you always answer questions by asking another?' the reply given was, 'Who told you that?' Therefore, make sure that you answer the set question, although there may be other questions that arise out of this for further study that you might want to highlight in your conclusion. As a first principle you must answer the set question and not the question that you had hoped for in the exam or essay.

Do not leave the examiner feeling like the person who interviews a politician and goes away with the impression that the important issues have been sidestepped.

EXAMPLE   Discuss why managers need to understand the environment when designing and managing organizations.

Some directly relevant points:

- The more complex the environment the greater the need for boundary spanning and buffering activities.
- The stability of the environment influences which organization structure and design might be most effective.
- Organizations need to adapt to political and social values and demands and so managers need to monitor the environment and develop appropriate structures.
- Uncertain environments can be better managed if the organization tries to gain control over needed resources...

Some less relevant points:

- The organization's domain consists of products, suppliers and customers.
- The organizational life cycle model has five stages, which are...

Although some of the points in the second list may be relevant overall, they are not as directly relevant to the question. You might mention that organizations need to understand and evaluate their domain – but you do not need to describe all the elements in the domain.

> *Be ready to resist the wealth of fascinating material at your disposal that is not directly relevant to your question.*

Missing your Question

A student bitterly complained after an exam that the topic he had revised so thoroughly had not been tested in the exam. The first response to that is that students should always cover enough topics to avoid selling themselves short in the exam – the habit of 'question spotting' is always a risky game to play. However, the reality in the anecdotal example was that the question the student was looking for was there, but he had not seen it. He had expected the question to be couched in certain words and he could not find these when he scanned the questions in blind panic. Therefore, the simple lesson is always read over the questions carefully, slowly and thoughtfully. This practice is time well spent.

> *You can miss the question if you restrict yourself to looking for a set form of words and if you do not read over all the words carefully.*

Underline the key words in the question

This will help you understand what the examiner is asking you to do.

> *If you read over the question several times you should be aware of all the key words and will begin to sense the connections between the ideas, and will envisage the possible directions you should take in your response.*

Take the following humorous example:

(a) What is that on the road ahead?
(b) What is that on the road, a head?

Question (a) calls for the identification of an object (what is that?), but question (b) has converted this into an object that suggests there has been a decapitation! Ensure therefore that you understand the direction the question is pointing you towards so that you do not go off at a tangent. One word in the question that is not properly attended to can throw you completely off track as in the following example:

(a) Discuss whether the love of money is the root of all evil.
(b) Discuss whether money is the root of all evil.

These are two completely different questions as (a) suggests that the real problem with money is inherent in faulty human use – that is, money itself may not be a bad thing if it is used as a servant and not a master. Whereas (b) may suggest that behind every evil act that has ever been committed, money is likely to have been implicated somewhere in the motive.

Pursue a Critical Approach

In degree courses you are usually expected to write critically rather than merely descriptively, although it may be necessary to use some minimal descriptive substance as the raw material for your debate.

EXAMPLE   Evaluate the evidence whether the American astronauts really walked on the moon, or whether this was a stage-managed hoax in a studio.

Arguments for studio hoax:

* Why is the flag blowing on moon?
* Explain the shadows
* Why are there no stars?
* Why is there little dust blowing at landing?
* Can humans survive passing through the radiation belt?

Arguments for walking on the moon:

* Communicates with laser reflectors left on moon
* Retrieved rocks show patterns that are not earthly

- How could such a hoax be protected?
- American activities were monitored by Soviets
- Plausible explanations for arguments against walking

Given that the question is about a critical evaluation of the evidence, you would need to address the issues one by one from both standpoints. What you should not do is digress into a tangent about the physical characteristics of the Beagle space ship or the astronauts' suits. Neither should you be drawn into a lengthy description of lunar features and contours even if you have in-depth knowledge of these.

Analyse the Parts

In an effective sports team the end product is always greater than the sum of the parts. Similarly, a good essay cannot be constructed without reference to the parts. Furthermore, the parts will arise as you break down the question into the components it suggests to you. Although the breaking down of a question into components is not sufficient for an excellent essay, it is a necessary starting point.

> *To achieve a good response to an exam or essay question, aim to integrate all the individual issues presented in a manner that gives shape and direction to your efforts.*

EXAMPLE 1   Discuss whether the preservation and restoration of listed buildings is justified.

Two parts to this question are clearly suggested – preservation and restoration, and you would need to do justice to each in your answer. Other issues that arise in relation to these are left for you to suggest and discuss. Examples might be finance, prioritization, poverty, beauty, culture, modernization, heritage and tourism.

EXAMPLE 2   Evaluate the advantages and disadvantages of giving students course credit for participation in experiments.

This is a straightforward question in that you have two major sections – advantages and disadvantages. You are left with the choice of the issues that you wish to address, and you can arrange these in the order you prefer. Your aim should be to ensure that you do not have a lopsided view of this even if you feel quite strongly one way or the other.

EXAMPLE 3   Trace in a critical manner Western society's changing attitudes to the corporal punishment of children.

In this case you might want to consider the role of governments, the church, schools, parents and the media. However, you will need to have some reference points to the past as you are asked to address the issue of change. There would also be scope to look at where the strongest influences for change arise and where the strongest resistance comes from. You might argue that the changes have been dramatic or evolutionary.

Give yourself plenty of practice at thinking of questions in this kind of way – both with topics on and not on your course. Topics not on your course that really interest you may be a helpful way to 'break you in' to this critical way of thinking.

Luchins and Learning Sets

In a series of experiments, Luchins allowed children to learn how to solve a problem that involved pouring water from and into a series of jugs of various sizes and shapes. He then gave them other problems that could be solved by following the same sequence. However, when he later gave them another problem that could be solved through a simpler sequence, they went about solving it through the previously learned procedure. In this case the original approach was more difficult but it had become so set in the children's minds that they were blinded to the shorter, more direct route.

EXAMPLE   How much did the wealthy Scottish man leave behind?

The story is told of a wealthy Scottish man who died, and no one in his village knew how much he had left behind. The issue was debated and gossiped about for some time, but one man claimed that he knew how much the man had left. He teased all the debaters and gossips in the village night after night. Eventually he let his big secret out, and the answer was that the rich man had left 'all of it' behind! No one in the village had been able to work out the mischievous man's little ruse because of the convergent thinking style they used. Some exam questions may require you to be divergent in the way you think (i.e. not just one obvious solution to the problem). This may mean being like a detective in the way you investigate and problem solve. The only difference is that you may need to set up the problem as well as the solution!

> *Get into the habit of 'stepping sideways' and looking at questions from several angles. The best way to do this is by practice, e.g. on previous exam papers.*

Checklist – ensuring that questions are understood before being fully addressed

✓ Read over the chosen question several times
✓ Underline the key words and see the connections between ideas
✓ Check that you have not omitted any important aspect or point of emphasis
✓ Ensure that you do not wrongly impose preconceived expectations on the question
✓ Break the question into parts (dismantle and rebuild)

You may be able to add further points to this list based on your own experience.

When Asked to Discuss

Students often ask how much of their own opinion they should include in an essay. In a discussion, when you raise one issue, another one can arise out of it. One tutor used to introduce his lectures by saying that he was going to 'unpack' the arguments. When you unpack an object (such as a new desk that has to be assembled), you first remove the overall packaging, such as a large box, and then proceed to remove the covers from all the component parts. After that you attempt to assemble all the parts, according to the given design, so that they hold together in the intended manner. In a discussion your aim should be not just to identify and define all the parts that contribute, but also to show where they fit (or don't fit) into the overall picture.

Although the word 'discuss' implies some allowance for your opinion, remember that this should be informed opinion rather than groundless speculation. Also, there must be direction, order, structure and end project.

Checklist – features of a response to a 'discuss' question

✓ Contains a chain of issues that lead into each other in sequence
✓ Clear shape and direction is unfolded in the progression of the argument
✓ Underpinned by reference to findings and certainties
✓ Identification of issues where doubt remains
✓ Tone of argument may be tentative but should not be vague

If a Critique is Requested

One example that might help clarify what is involved in a critique is the hotly debated topic of the physical punishment of children. It would be important in the interest of balance and fairness to present all sides and shades of the argument. You would then look at whether there is available evidence to support each argument, and you might introduce issues that have been coloured by prejudice, tradition, religion and legislation. It would be an aim to identify emotional arguments, arguments based on intuition and to get down to those arguments that really have solid evidence-based support. Finally you would want to flag up where the strongest evidence appears to lie, and you should also identify issues that appear to be inconclusive. It would be expected that you should, if possible, arrive at some certainties.

EXERCISE

Write your own summary checklist for the features of a critique. You can either summarize the above points, use your own points or a mixture of the two.

✓ ....
✓ ....
✓ ....
✓ ....
✓ ....

If Asked to Compare and Contrast

When asked to compare and contrast, you should be thinking in terms of similarities and differences. You should ask what the two issues share in common, and what features of each are distinct. Your preferred strategy for tackling this might be to work first through all the similarities and then through all the contrasts (or vice versa). On the other hand, work through a similarity and contrast, followed by another similarity and contrast, etc.

EXAMPLE   Compare and contrast the uses of tea and coffee as beverages.

Similarities:

- Usually drunk hot
- Can be drunk without food
- Can be taken with a snack or meal
- Can be drunk with milk
- Can be taken with honey, sugar or sweeteners
- Both contain caffeine
- Both can be addictive

Contrasts:

- Differences in taste
- Tea perhaps preferred at night
- Differences in caffeine content
- Coffee more bitter
- Coffee sometimes taken with cream or whiskey
- Each perhaps preferred with different foods
- Coffee preferred for hangover

> *When you compare and contrast you should aim to paint a true picture of the full 'landscape'.*

Whenever Evaluation is Requested

EXAMPLE   TV soap opera director.

Imagine that you are a TV director for a popular soap opera. You have observed in recent months that you have lost some viewers to an alternative soap opera on a rival channel. All is not yet lost because you still have a loyal hard core of viewers who have remained faithful. Your programme has been broadcasted for ten years and there has, until recently, been little change in viewing figures. The rival programme has used some fresh ideas and new actors and has a big novelty appeal. It will take time to see if their level of viewing can be sustained, but you run the risk that you might lose some more viewers at least in the short term. On the other hand, with some imagination you might be able to attract some viewers back. However, there have been some recent murmurings about aspects of the programme being stale, repetitive and predictable. You have been given the task of evaluating the programme to see if you can ascertain why you have retained the faithful but lost other viewers, and what you could do to improve the programme without compromising the aspects that work. In your task you might want to review past features (retrospective), outline present features (perspective) and envisage positive future changes (prospective). This illustration may provoke you to think about how you might approach a question that asks you to evaluate some theory or concept in your own academic field of study. Some summary points to guide you are presented below:

- Has the theory/concept stood the test of time?
- Is there a supportive evidence base that would not easily be overturned?
- Are there questionable elements that have been or should be challenged?
- Does more recent evidence point to a need for modification?
- Is the theory/concept robust and likely to be around for the foreseeable future?
- Could it be strengthened through being merged with other theories/concepts?

It should be noted that the words presented in the above examples might not always be the exact words that will appear on your exam script – e.g. you might find 'analyse', or 'outline' or 'investigate', etc. The best advice is to check over your past exam papers and familiarize yourself with the words that are most recurrent.

In summary, this Part has been designed to give you reference points to measure where you are at in your studies, and to help you map out the way ahead in manageable increments. It should now be clear that learning should not merely be a mechanical exercise, such as just memorizing and reproducing study material. Quality learning also involves making connections between ideas, thinking at a deeper level by attempting to understand your material, developing a critical approach to learning, and being able to apply your knowledge or to understand how it applies to organizations. This cannot be achieved without the discipline of preparation for lectures, seminars and exams, or without learning to structure your material (headings and subheadings) and to set each unit of learning within its overall context in your subject and programme. An important device in learning is to develop the ability to ask questions (whether written, spoken or silent). Another useful device in learning is to illustrate your material and use examples that will help make your study fun, memorable and vivid. It is useful to set problems for yourself that will allow you to think through solutions and therefore enhance the quality of your learning.

On the one hand there are the necessary disciplined procedures such as preparation before each learning activity and consolidation afterwards. It is also vital to keep your subject materials in organized folders so that you can add/extract/replace materials when you need to. On the other hand there is the need to develop personal qualities such as feeding your confidence, fuelling your motivation and turning stress responses to your advantage. This chapter has presented strategies to guide you through finding the balance between these organized and dynamic aspects of academic life.

Your aim should be to become an 'all round student' who engages in and benefits from all the learning activities available to you (lectures, seminars, tutorials, computing, labs, discussions, library work, etc.), and to develop all the academic and personal skills that will put you in the driving seat to academic achievement. It will be motivating and confidence building for you, if you can recognize the value of these qualities, both across your academic programme and beyond graduation to the world of work. They will also serve you well in your continued commitment to life-long learning.

Adaptability cultures

value innovation, creativity, risk-taking.

Advanced manufacturing technology (AMT)

innovations in technology, manufacturing processes and systems, for example, sustainable manufacturing – maintaining environmental quality;

supply chain management – networks of suppliers and manufacturers;

computer-aided design (CAD) – of products (cars, airplanes, etc.);

computer-aided manufacturing (CAM) – facilitates automation;

robotics – programmed electro-mechanical devices and systems used in manufacturing, e.g., for welding, painting, etc.;

computer integrated manufacturing (CIM) – a shared database to integrate all aspects of the business (sales production, distribution, etc.);

nanotechnology – designing and manufacturing extremely small electronic circuits and machines.

Agency theory

principals are dependent on agents to achieve goals and need to ensure those agents will act in the best interest of the principal.

Boundary spanning

ways in which the organization tries to monitor its environment, e.g. by getting information about market changes, new developments in materials or processes, and new legislation.

Buffering	how the organization protects itself from environmental uncertainties, and maintains continued operation, e.g., by training people to become qualified workers in case of a labour shortage, to stockpile or buy a supplier company to ensure raw materials are available.
Bureaucratic cultures	value consistency, control, conformity.
Centralization	decisions made by senior management.
Clan cultures	value commitment, teamwork, participation.
Competitive advantage	how an organization competes with others through a more effective and efficient utilization of resources (physical, financial, etc.). This also involves maximizing the organization's core competencies – the skills, abilities and expertise of its employees.
Control	putting the mechanisms in place to ensure that performance meets the required goals and standards.
Decentralization	decisions made at all levels in the organization.
Differentiation	differences within the organization, also known as the division of labour. The way authority, tasks and positions are divided and then grouped together to achieve goals, e.g., the number of levels in the hierarchy, functions, departments and sub-units.
Disciplinary power	a form of power existing, and expressed, in all social relationships and practices.
Emergent change	bottom-up change often adapting to problems or issues as they arise.

Evolutionary change	occurs over a long period of time, e.g., gradual growth or decline.
External adaptation	how the organization manages it's environment.
Formalization	the degree to which roles, responsibilities, rules, policies, communication and operating procedures, etc. are defined.
Generalization	broadly defined tasks and roles. Employees require a wide range of skills, knowledge and expertise.
Hegemony	when groups give spontaneous consent to their domination by others.
Incremental change	building on the current situation to introduce change through a series of steps, e.g., improving a product. Often involves part of the organization.
Information technology (IT)	the equipment, systems, knowledge and skills used in the acquisition, storage, use and dissemination of information (hardware, software, networks, support services, etc.).
Innovation	developing new products, services, technology and/or work processes.
Integration	the way in which work and actions of the various parts of the organization are coordinated.
Knowledge management	the systematic capture, organization, formalization and dissemination of the knowledge, expertise and experience of employees.

Management information systems (MIS)	computer-based information systems and databases used to support management planning, scheduling and decision making.
Mission cultures	value mission, vision and goal achievement.
Mutual adjustment	few standard procedures. Employees use their judgement and initiative to deal with events and problems.
Networking	computer-based information networks allowing people to share information.
Organization culture	the basic set of assumptions, beliefs, values, norms, stories, rites, ceremonies, artifacts and symbols within the organization, that influence the way things are done.
Organization structure	how tasks, resources and people are formally grouped together to achieve organizational goals. Structure consists of a number of structural elements or design factors.
Organizational change	moving from a current to a desired state.
Organizational conflict	when two or more groups and individuals compete or struggle to achieve their goals over others.
Organizational design	the choices made about which combination of structural elements will best meet organizational goals.
Organizational domain	the organization's field of activity: its products, services, markets, customers, financial institutions, suppliers, etc.

Organizational environment	the general forces or elements existing outside the organization, but which might have an influence on its survival and operation.
Organizational learning	improving the organization's, teams' and individual employees' ability to acquire and create new knowledge in order to improve organizational performance.
Organizational sectors	specific elements within the environment, e.g., technology.
Planned change	top-down managed change.
Politics	behaviour and actions designed to increase influence, power and control over resources, as a means of achieving one's own goals.
Power	when one person or group can influence another person or group to do something they might not otherwise do.
Radical change	involves a major shift in the way of thinking resulting in the organization reinventing itself so that the structure, culture, service delivery, etc. is different to the past, e.g., moving from a functional to a matrix structure, Apple expanding from personal computers to entertainment (iPod, iTunes). Often involves the whole organization.
Revolutionary change	occurs over a short period of time and has a major impact, e.g., the

Department of Motor Vehicles introducing an online system.

Self-surveillance

a form of power and control that occurs when we monitor our own behaviour as a result of a number of surveillance techniques (e.g., evaluations, being trained how to behave at work).

Specialization

work is organized into narrowly defined tasks and specific areas of expertise. Employees are specialists in particular fields.

Stakeholders

people (individuals, groups and institutions) who have an interest or influence on the organization, e.g., shareholders, customers, suppliers, legislators.

Standardization

standard procedures are used to control activities and operations.

Strategic contingencies

power is based on an ability to deal with uncertainty and resolve critical organizational problems.

Strategy

the plan, decisions and actions identified as being necessary to achieving organizational goals.

Theory Z

a blend of Japanese and American cultural values including individual responsibility, collective decision making, long-term employment.

references

Argyris, C. and Schön, D. (1978) *Organizational Learning*. Reading, MA: Addison-Wesley.

Berger, P. L. and Luckmann, T. (1966) *The Social Construction of Reality: A Treatise in the Sociology of Knowledge*. Garden City, NY: Doubleday.

Boulding, K. E. (1956) 'General systems theory – the skeleton of science', *Management Science*, 2: 197–208.

Burns, T. and Stalker, G. M. (1966) *The Management of Innovation*. London: Tavistock Publications.

Burrell, G. and Morgan, G. (1979) *Sociological Paradigms and Organizational Analysis*. London: Heineman.

Child, J. (2005) *Organization: Contemporary Principles and Practice*. Oxford: Blackwell.

Cooper, R. and Burrell, G. (1988) 'Modernism, postmodernism and organizational analysis: an introduction', *Organization Studies*, 9: 91–112.

Crozier, M. (1964) *The Bureaucratic Phenomenon*. London: Tavistock.

Daft, R. L. (2007) *Organization Theory and Design*, 9th edn. Thomson: Southwestern.

Deal, T. and Kennedy, A. (1982) *Corporate Cultures: The Rites and Rituals of Corporate Life*. Reading, MA: Addison-Wesley.

Denison, D. R. (1990) *Corporate Culture and Organizational Effectiveness*. New York: Wiley.

Fayol, H. (1949) *General and Industrial Management*. London: Pitman (first published in 1919).

Ganzer, V. J. (1968) 'Effects of audience presence and test anxiety on learning and retention in a serial learning situation', *Journal of Personality and Social Psychology*, 8: 194–99.

Gouldner, A. W. (1954) *Patterns of Industrial Bureaucracy*. Glencoe, IL: Free Press.

Greiner, L. (1972) 'Evolution and revolution as organizations grow', *Harvard Business Review*, 50: 37–46.

Harvey, D. (1990) *The Condition of Postmodernity*. Cambridge, MA: Blackwell.

Hickson, David J., Hinings, C. R., Lee, C. A., Schneck, R. E. and Pennings, J. M. (1971) 'A strategic contingencies theory of intra-organizational power', *Administrative Science Quarterly*, 16: 216–29.

Hofstede, G. (1985) 'The interaction between national and organizational value systems', *Journal of Management Studies*, 22: 347–57.

Hofstede, G. (2001) *Culture's Consequences: Comparing Values, Behaviors, Institutions and Organizations,* 2nd edn. Thousand Oaks, CA: Sage.

Jones, G. R. (2007) *Organizational Theory, Design and Change,* 5th edn. Englewood Cliffs, NJ: Prentice-Hall.

Kotter, J. (1996) *Leading Change.* Boston, MA: Harvard Business School Press.

Lave, J. and Wenger, E. (1991) *Situated Learning: Legitimate Peripheral Participation.* Cambridge: Cambridge University Press.

Lawrence, P. R. and Lorsch, J. W. (1967) *Organization and Environment: Managing Differentiation and Integration.* Boston, Division of Research, Graduate School of Business Administration, Harvard University.

Lewin, K. (1951) *Field-Theory in Social Science.* New York: Harper and Row.

Luchins, A. S. (1942) 'Mechanisms in problem solving: the effects of *Einstellung',* *Psychological Monographs* 54 (248).

Lyotard, J. F. (1984) *The Postmodern Condition: A Report on Knowledge.* Minneapolis: University of Minnesota Press.

March, J. G. (1991) 'Exploration and exploitation in organized learning', *Organization Science,* 2: 71–87.

March, J. G. and Simon, H. A. (1958) *Organizations.* New York: John Wiley.

Marx, K. (1867) *Capital Vol 1.* Hamburg: Verlag von Otto Meissner.

Mintzberg, H. (1978) 'Patterns in strategy formation', *Management Science,* 24: 934–48.

Mintzberg, H. (1994) 'The fall and rise of strategic planning', *Harvard Business Review,* 72(1): 107–14.

Nonaka, I. and Takeuchi, H. (1995) *The Knowledge-Creating Company.* New York: Oxford University Press.

Ouchi, W. G. (1979) 'A conceptual framework for the design of organizational control mechanisms', *Management Science,* 25: 833–48.

Ouchi, W. G. (1981) *Theory Z.* Reading, MA: Addison-Wesley.

Parsons, T. (1951) *The Social System.* Free Press.

Perrow, C. (1967) 'A framework for comparative organizational analysis', *American Sociological Review,* 32(2): 194–208.

Peters, T. J. and Waterman, R. H. (1982) *In Search of Excellence: Lessons from America's Best Run Companies.* New York: Harper Row.

Pfeffer, J. (1981) *Power in Organizations.* Boston: Pitman.

Pfeffer, J. and Salancik, G. R. (1978) *The External Control of Organizations: A Resource Dependence Perspective.* New York: Harper and Row.

Piore, M. J. and Sabel, C. F. (1984) *The Second Industrial Divide: Possibilities for Prosperity.* New York: Basic Books.

Polanyi, M. (1966) *The Tacit Dimension.* London: Routledge and Kegan Paul.

Pondy, L. R. (1967) 'Organizational conflict: concepts and models', *Administrative Science Quarterly,* 12: 296–320.

Porter, M. E. (1980) *Competitive Strategy: Techniques for Analyzing Industries and Competitors*. New York: Free Press.

Porter, M. (1985) *Competitive Advantage: Creating and Sustaining Superior Performance*. New York: Free Press.

Reed, M. and Hughes, M. (eds) (1992) *Rethinking Organizations*. London: Sage.

Sarbin, T. R. and Kitsuse, J. J. (eds) (1994) *Constructing the Social*. Inquiries in Social Construction Series. London: Sage.

Schein, E. H. (1985) *Organizational Culture and Leadership*. San Francisco: Jossey Bass.

Schein, E. H. (1992) *Organizational Culture and Leadership*, 2nd edn. San Francisco: Jossey-Bass.

Scott, R. W. (1992) *Organizations: Rational, Natural, and Open Systems*, 3rd edn. Englewood Cliffs, NJ: Prentice-Hall.

Senge, P. (1990) *The Fifth Discipline: The Art and Practice of the Learning Organization*. New York: Doubleday.

Smith, A. (1776) *An Inquiry into the Nature and Causes of the Wealth of Nations*. Edinburgh: Strachan and Cadell.

Taylor, F. W. (1911) *The Principles of Scientific Management*. New York: Harper.

Thompson, J. (1967) *Organizations in Action*. New York: McGraw-Hill.

Trice, H. M. and Beyer, J. M. (1984) 'Studying organizational cultures through rites and ceremonials', *Academy of Management Review*, 9: 653–9.

Trist, E. L. and Bamforth, K. W. (1951) 'Some social and psychological consequences of the long wall method of coal getting', *Human Relations*, 4: 3–38.

Watson, T. J. (2001) *In Search of Management: Culture, Chaos and Control in Managerial Word*, revised edn. London: Thompson Business Press.

Watson, T. J. (2006) *Organising and Managing Work*, 2nd edn. Harlow, Essex: Pearson Education.

Weber, M. (1947) *The Theory of Social and Economic Organization* (eds A. H. Henderson and Talcott Parsons). Glencoe, Il: Free Press (first published in 1924).

Weick, K. E. (1979) *The Social Psychology of Organizing*. Reading, MA: Addison Wesley (first published 1969).

Woodward, J. (1965) *Industrial Organization: Theory and Practice*. London: Oxford University Press.

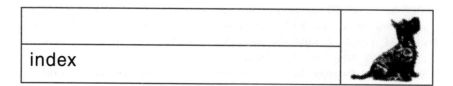

index

Please note that page references to non-textual information such as Figures or Tables are in *italic* print